Tap Into
the
Great Lakes

A Guide to the Brewpubs & Microbreweries of
Michigan, Illinois, Indiana,
Ohio, & Wisconsin

John Bice

Thunder Bay Press

Tap into the Great Lakes ©1999 by John Bice

Printed in the United States of America

03 02 01 00 99   5 4 3 2 1

ISBN 1-882376-67-6

Cover design by Kathryn Darnell

Holt, Michigan

CONTENTS

*"Of beer, an enthusiast has said that
it could never be bad, but that
some brands might be better than others."*
— A. A. Milne

INTRODUCTION

*T*his project began in 1997. At that time, I had no inkling of the challenge that lay ahead. Many of the breweries listed in this book did not exist when I started. It has been an effort to keep up with the microbrewery explosion that has taken place. Although it may look as though the majority of the microbrewery growth in the Great Lakes region is behind us, the industry remains in flux even today. Over the next few years we will surely see new brewery openings, as well as some scattered closings. Nevertheless, one thing is certain: there has never been a better time to be a beer lover in the Midwest. The states of Michigan, Ohio, Indiana, Illinois, and Wisconsin offer over 200 breweries for our drinking and dining pleasure. Represented among them are some of the best breweries in the country, and I believe a few of the finest beers in the world.

My beer background is likely a very common one. I was weaned on American light lagers, soon moved on to Canadian lagers, and then discovered imported beer from around the world. That is when the fun began. Over the years I have sampled thousands of beers from every available style. Most recently I had the opportunity to visit the birth countries of my personal favorite styles of beer. I consider my time in Europe to have been a nearly religious journey of discovery.

While Europe does offer a treasure-trove of excellent beers, the same can be said for beers brewed here in the United States. The American brewing tradition is finally beginning to reflect our country's diversity. In no other single country can you so easily find German, British, Belgian, Scottish, Irish, American, and other world beer styles–sometimes all offered by a single brewery!

This new diversity has spawned breweries of all types, some that specialize in brewing traditional beers from specific countries, and others that look to add an American flair to traditional styles. Through the use of American hop varieties, we have introduced new variations of beer that are now being imitated by brewers of other countries. Definitely an exciting time.

Unfortunately, the news is not all good. The microbrewery renaissance has demonstrated no immunity to the American propensity for over-commercialization and trendy fads. Consequently, clever packaging and marketing are often conceived before, and take priority over, the quality of the beer. "Theme" breweries abound, using their microbrewed beer as yet another gimmick to bring people in. All told, the quality of the beer does suffer. Too many breweries in the Great Lakes region, and elsewhere, fall into a pattern of brewing their beers to the extreme light end of the spectrum. These beers are often well made and "clean," with no off flavors, but are not brewed to stimulate and inspire. Often their goal is simply to not offend the uninitiated. These beers tend to only hint at the characteristics of the styles they are said to represent, and lack distinction. Strangely, this practice is often defended by blaming the palate of American beer drinkers. Breweries cite the fact that in their area most people are light lager drinkers. Of course they are; most beer drinkers all over the country fall into that category, and yet the majority of the most successful microbreweries are those that brew very distinctive and true-to-style beers. Examples are numerous. Blaming the palate of the beer consumer is simply without merit.

While I made an effort to visit every brewery in the Great Lakes, and sample as many beers as humanly possible, I certainly have not tried them all. Some breweries I could not visit in the time frame I was constrained by, and my experience with many was limited to only one or two visits. I am sure that along the way I have missed many excellent beers, and probably hit a few breweries that were having a bad beer day. Also, my home state of Michigan has an admitted advantage over the other states in that I was able to be much more thorough, visiting some of my favorite breweries again and again. Had I been able to give all the Great Lakes states that same level of attention, I am certain there would be a few more "Best of Great Lakes" breweries. That some deserving breweries have probably been overlooked in no way diminishes the quality of the breweries I have singled out.

The decision to write this book grew from my own frustration with the lack of a clear and concise guide to Great Lakes microbreweries. The bigger national microbreweries receive considerable attention, as do a select few Great Lakes breweries. However, what had been missing was a single source providing information on the rich diversity of breweries scattered all over the Midwest. It is my hope that this guidebook effectively fills that previously overlooked niche. My primary goals for this book are twofold. First, I wanted to provide the most comprehensive single source listing and collection of information available on Midwest microbreweries, providing the traveler, or dedicated pub-crawler, an easy path to regional microbrewed beer. Second, I tried to distinguish between the average breweries and those making truly spectacular beer. Right here in the Great Lakes states it is possible to find breweries producing beers that rival those made anywhere in the world. You just have to know where to look. The ultimate goal of this book is to provide the means to find these hidden treasures. It is my hope that this guide will direct you to a brewery you might have otherwise missed, and introduce you to a few new favorite beers.

– John Bice
August 1999

HOW TO USE THIS BOOK

*L*arge breweries have one advantage over small-scale microbreweries: consistency. Mega-breweries are exceedingly good at making their beers taste the same from one batch to the next; they may churn out one ill-conceived beer after another, but at least they have excellent consistency. Microbreweries, due to a number of reasons, can have difficulty achieving that same level of consistency. Often the same beer will vary noticeably from batch to batch. If a beer varied in quality, I rated the best sample.

Beers are rated according to two criteria. First, they are judged based on the styles they are said to represent, while allowing a great deal of freedom for creativity and distinctiveness. I look for a beer that either "nails" the style by modeling a classic example, or a beer that exhibits the fundamentals of a style while adding its own flair and creative interpretation. Beers are further judged on how well they compare to other examples of that style brewed in the Great Lakes Region.

- **Fair**–Hints at the traits common in the style it represents.
- •• **Good**–Typical of this style as brewed in the Great Lakes states.
- ••• **Very Good**–Worth ordering a second pint of.
- •••• **Excellent**–Excites, inspires, and satisfies. These are beers to be sought after.

Please note that some beers are unrated because I was not able to sample them all.

BEST OF THE GREAT LAKES BREWERY AWARD

 This symbol appears next to every brewery that has been selected as one of the finest breweries in the Great Lakes. The beers at each of these breweries have been judged to be of superior quality, demonstrating the brewery's commitment to producing the finest beers possible. They all exemplify the original purpose of the American microbrewery renaissance: to provide excellent and distinctive beers that are far from ordinary. Any of these establishments are well worth a detour or even a special trip to sample their efforts.

RECOMMENDED BREWERY

This icon appears next to breweries that have met the critical criteria of brewing above average beer. In addition to brewing compelling beers, many offer an interesting atmosphere and great food. Each one of them is worth a visit.

PRICE RATING SYSTEM

Inexpensive: Easy to eat for around $5 per person.
Average: Typical brewpub pricing. Expect sandwiches, pub grub, and most entrees to be under $10.
Average to Expensive: Many entrees hover around the $10 range.
Expensive: Most entrees over $10.

LOCATING THE BREWERIES

The breweries in this book are organized by location. If you want to know where to find a good beer in a particular city or town, look up the section for your state in the Table of Contents. Then go to that section and look up any city in alphabetical order. If you're looking for a particular brewery and want to know where it's located, use the index, where breweries are listed in alphabetical order.

BREWERIES OF ILLINOIS

ILLINOIS "BEST OF GREAT LAKES" BREWERIES

ADDITIONAL RECOMMENDED ILLINOIS BREWERIES

Arlington Heights, Illinois
O'GRADY'S BREWERY & PUB

372 East Golf Road, Arlington Heights, IL 60005; phone 847-640-0600
Type: Brewpub
Near: Arlington Heights Road in the "Cosmetic Center" roadside mall
Nearby City: See Chicago
Opens: 11 a.m. Monday-Saturday; 10 a.m. Sunday
Prices: Average
Opening Date: May 1996
Most Popular Beer: Chicago Fire
Brewing System: 10 barrel, Specific Mechanical

BEER LIST
Year Round:
   Magnificent Mild (Light Lager)
•• **Haymarket Pilsner**–Perleand Saaz hops. Nice dry finish, good hop character.
••• **Smokehouse Porter**–Full-bodied and malty up front with a roasty and hoppy finish.
••• **Stockyard Stout**–Roastier and bigger bodied than the porter. Chocolaty malt finish.
•• **Board of Trade Wheat**–A lovely, cloudy, unfiltered wheat.
••• **Chicago Fire** (Red Ale)–Slight smoky character and a satisfyingly balanced malt/hop finish.
Seasonal:
• **Blacksmith Bitter**–Named for Thomas O'Grady, a blacksmith in Chicago during the late nineteenth century. Mildly buttery.
•• **Dubbel Bock**–Ruby red and malty sweet with a strong alcohol component.
•••• **St. Brigid's Strong Ale**–Their 100th brew. Flavors include a touch of scotch, cinnamon, coriander, orange peel, and honey. A nicely complex beer, with a warming alcohol presence.

BREWERY NOTES
Much better than average brewpub. Live music on weekends. Family restaurant/pub atmosphere. Good food and beer.

Aurora, Illinois
AMERICA'S BREWPUB–
WALTER PAYTON'S ROUNDHOUSE

205 North Broadway, Aurora, IL 60507; phone 630-264-BREW
Web Address: www.americasbrewpub.com
Type: Microbrewery and Restaurant
Near: New York Street
Opens: 11 a.m. Monday-Saturday; noon Sunday
Prices: Expensive
Opening Date: March 1996
Most Popular Beer: Honey Wheat Ale
Brewing System: 30 barrel, DME

BEER LIST
- **Honey Wheat Ale**
- **Aurora Amber Ale**
- **Payton Pilsner**–Saaz hops
- **Sweeney Stout**

BREWERY NOTES
Live music on Friday and Saturday. You'll need reservations on the weekends if you plan on visiting the restaurant. Otherwise you can just walk up to any one of the several bars.

The Aurora Roundhouse is reportedly the oldest existing limestone roundhouse in the nation. The "look" is that of a stadium. The center "playing field" is an enormous open-air beer garden, complete with a small putting green and large outdoor fireplaces. It is absolutely huge. Other highlights include the Walter Payton Museum and a cognac/cigar bar. Worth a visit if just for the spectacle of it all. Six-packs available to go.

Carbondale, Illinois
COPPER DRAGON BREWING COMPANY

700 East Grand, Carbondale, IL 62901; phone: 618-549-2319
Web Address: www.midwest.net/tms/copper
Type: Brewpub
Near: Wall Street
Opens: 4 p.m. Monday-Saturday; closed Sundays
Prices: Average to Expensive
Opening Date: 1996
Most Popular Beer: Oatmeal Stout
Brewing System: 7 barrel, DME

BEER LIST
  Pale Ale
  Weiss Bier
  Blonde Ale
  Scotch Ale–7.5% alcohol
  Porter
  Oatmeal Stout

BREWERY NOTES
Located in an old movie theater.

Chicago, Illinois

For Chicago breweries, also see these nearby cities: Arlington Heights, Berwyn, Downers Grove, Flossmoor, Glen Ellyn, Lake Barrington, Libertyville, Lincolnshire, Naperville, South Barrington, Villa Park, Warrenville, and Westmont.

Chicago, Illinois
BREWING COMPANY NO. 9

2350 North Clybourn Avenue, Chicago IL 60614; phone 773-472-9999
Type: Microbrewery and Taproom/Brew-on-Premises
Near: South of Fullerton
Opens: 5 p.m. Wednesday-Friday; noon on weekends
Opening Date: February 1996
Most Popular Beers: Huckleberry Brown and The Chief
Brewing System: Six single-barrel systems

BEER LIST
  Huckleberry Brown
  The Chief (American-style Pale Ale)
  Miami Weiss (Bavarian-style Wheat)
  Northern Common (California Common)
  Grouper (English Pale)–Modeled after Bass ale
  Canadian Golden
  New England Chestnut Brown (English Brown)

BREWERY NOTES
12 beers on tap, over 70 different recipes.

Chicago, Illinois
GOOSE ISLAND BEER COMPANY

1800 West Fulton, Chicago, IL 60612; phone 800-466-7363
E-mail: info@gooseisland.com
Web Address: www.gooseisland.com

Type: Regional Brewery
Near: Ashland Avenue, corner of Fulton and Wood
Open: 8 a.m.-5 p.m. Monday-Friday
Opening Date: November 1995
Most Popular Beer: Honker's Ale
Brewing System: 100 barrel

BEER LIST

•••• **Honker's Ale**–Spicy and caramelly nose. Toasted and caramel-like malt qualities, married with a mildly spicy and dry finish. An easy drinking and complexly flavorful ale.

••• **Hexnut Brown Ale**

•••• **I.P.A.**–The perfect American I.P.A., featuring an incredibly resinous hop nose and flavor. A hop playground in every bottle.

•••• **Blonde Ale**–Brewed with 20% wheat malt. Fuggles, Mt. Hood, and Northern Brewer hops. A lightly sour nose and palate, and smooth, almost creamy, mouthfeel. Surprisingly floral and spicy hop character, yet it remains very drinkable. Crisp and refreshing.

••• **Summertime Ale** (Kölsch)–Summer seasonal.

••• **Christmas Ale**–A unique brew every holiday season.

••• **Kilgubbin Red Ale** (Irish-style Red Ale)–Kilgubbin is the Gaelic name for "goose island," and is offered as a spring seasonal. Brewed with Liberty and Northern Brewer hops. Amber-red colored with a slightly prickly mouthfeel. It exhibits surprising suggestions of chocolate in the initial flavor, and a spicy zing in the finish, courtesy of a touch of malty rye. An interesting beer, and very unique.

BREWERY NOTES

Goose Island is among a select group of Midwest breweries that has achieved significant national recognition, and has deservingly won numerous awards for both their breweries and their beers. Their beers are bottle conditioned, and to the delight of many, are available outside of Illinois. Honker's Ale is available on draft at over 500 accounts in Chicago, and is a featured craft beer at Wrigley Field. See also the Goose Island Brewing Company, and Goose Island Wrigleyville, their brewpubs (also in Chicago).

Chicago, Illinois
GOOSE ISLAND BREWING COMPANY

1800 North Clybourn Avenue, Chicago, IL 60614
Phone: 312-915-0071
E-mail: info@gooseisland.com
Web Address: www.gooseisland.com
Type: Brewpub
Near: Sheffield
Opens: 11:30 a.m. weekdays; 11:00 a.m. weekends
Opening Date: 1988
Most Popular Beer: Honker's Ale
Brewing System: 10 Barrel
Prices: Average

BEER LIST

•••• **Honker's Ale**
••• **Hexnut Brown Ale**
•• **PMD Mild Ale**
•• **E.S.B.**–Skillfully balanced beer.
•• **Golden Goose Pilsner**–Nicely hopped and refreshing.
•• **Oatmeal Stout**–Thin bodied and roasty.
•••• **Bourbon County Stout**–Incredibly complex and intensely flavored stout.
    Full bodied and viscous. An excellent dessert beer.
•• **Kriek**–A good cherry ale, although it lacks much Belgian character.
••• **Baltic Porter**–A smooth mellow ale.
Plus too many seasonals to list

BREWERY NOTES

An outstanding brewpub that not only offers the flagship Goose Island beers, but also an incredible list of seasonal beers constantly changing throughout the year. In fact, in 1998 they brewed 100 different beers, covering a wide range of styles including many types seldom brewed in the states. I can't imagine a trip to Chicago that doesn't include a visit to Goose Island.

The atmosphere is a comfortable combination of pub and restaurant, with pool tables and TV. Cask ales are offered, as are brewmaster dinners, brewery tours, and even an MBA (Master of Beer Appreciation) degree program.

See also the Goose Island Beer Company, where the bottled beer is brewed, and Goose Island Wrigleyville, their newest brewpub next to Wrigley Field.

Chicago, Illinois
GOOSE ISLAND WRIGLEYVILLE

3535 North Clark Street, Chicago, IL 60657; phone 773-832-9040
E-mail: info@gooseisland.com/wrigley
Web Address: www.gooseisland.com
Type: Brewpub
Near: Wrigley Field
Opens: 4 p.m. Monday-Friday, 11 a.m. Saturday, Sunday, and Cub home
  games
Opening Date: April 1999
Most Popular Beer: Honker's Ale

BEER LIST
For a list of beers, see the Goose Island Beer Company, where their bottled beer is brewed, and Goose Island Brewing Company, their original brewpub.

BREWERY NOTES
Just steps away from historic Wrigley Field, it's hard to imagine a better location for a Chicago brewpub. With their 9 TVs (including 3 large projection screens), the brewpub will be close to utopia for any beer and baseball fan. All this plus beer that will put nearly any sports bar to shame.

Chicago, Illinois
HOPCATS RESTAURANT & BREWERY

2354 North Clybourn Avenue, Chicago, IL 60614; phone 773-868-4461
Web Address: www.hopcats.com
Type: Brewpub
Near: Fullerton
Opens: 11 a.m. Tuesday-Sunday; closed Monday except the Topcat Lounge, a bar that opens at 6 p.m.
Prices: Average
Opening Date: July 1998
Most Popular Beer: Oatmeal Pale Ale
Brewing System: 10 barrel, Liquid Assets

BEER LIST

Hopcats Honey Blonde Ale
Hopcats Montmarency Brown Ale–A Belgian brown ale made with Michigan cherries
Oatmeal Pale Ale
I.P.A.–Nugget hops for bittering, Goldings and Cascade for dry-hopping
No Jokes Blonde Ale
Rockin' Roggen–Bavarian dark rye
Heifer Stout (Milk Stout)
Belgian Ale–Specific style rotates seasonally
Wheat Ale–Specific style rotates seasonally

BREWERY NOTES

Upstairs is the "Topcat Lounge" open Monday-Friday, 6 p.m.-2 a.m.; Saturday noon-3 a.m.; and Sunday noon-2 a.m. Live music is featured on Tuesdays, Thursdays and Sundays. The basement houses "Let's Brew It," a homebrew supply store. Restaurant features recipes from around the world.

11

Chicago, Illinois
RIVER WEST BREWING COMPANY

925 West Chicago Avenue, Chicago, IL 60622; phone 312-226-3200
Type: Brewpub
Near: Halsted Street
Opens: 11 a.m. daily
Prices: Average
Opening Date: 1996
Brewing System: 15 barrel

BEER LIST
   Windy City Pilsner
   Red Fox Amber Ale
   Railroad Stout
   Berliner Weiss
   Maibock (Seasonal)
   Steam
   Whistle Stop Weiss
   I.P.A.
   Doubledecker Doppelbock

Chicago, Illinois
ROCK BOTTOM BREWERY #7

1 West Grand Avenue, Chicago, IL 60611; phone 312-755-9339
Web Address: www.rockbottom.com
Type: Brewpub
Near: Corner of State and Grand Avenue
Opens: 11:30 a.m. daily
Prices: Average to expensive
Opening Date: October 1995
Most Popular Beer: Chicago Gold
Brewing System: 12 barrel, J.V. Northwest

BEER LIST
  • **Chicago Gold**
  • **Walleye Wheat**
  • **Eric Red Ale**
  • **Brown Bear Brown**
  • **Terminal Stout**

BREWERY NOTES
Large Colorado based brewpub chain with many locations. Twelve or more specialty beers every year that vary seasonally. Generally 7-8 beers on tap at anyone time.

Downers Grove, Illinois
FOUNDERS HILL BREWING COMPANY

5200 Main Street, Downers Grove, IL 60515; phone 630-963-2739
Type: Brewpub
Near: Between Curtis and Maple Street
Nearby City: See Chicago
Opens: 11 a.m. Monday-Saturday; 3 p.m. Sunday
Prices: Average
Opening Date: June 1996
Most Popular Beer: Heritage Wheat
Brewing System: 15 barrel, Specific Mechanical

BEER LIST
- ••• **Heritage Wheat**–Brewed with 40% wheat and seasoned with Hallertau and Willamette hops.
- •••• **Pierce's Pale Ale**–Excellent English-style pale ale. East Kent Golding hops provide both bitterness and aroma.
- ••• **Scarlett's Raspberry Wheat**–Great raspberry nose. Nice tart berry flavor.
- •• **Hidden River Red Ale**–Willamette and Hallertau hops.
- •• **Blacksmith Stout** (Oatmeal Stout)
- ••• **Founders Light Lager**–Quite good for a low-calorie light lager, assuming that's a desirable beer.
- • **Downers Dopplebock**–Strong alcohol flavor and aroma, lacking in much malt complexity.
- •• **Traditions American Brown Ale**
  Mainstreet Maibock

BREWERY NOTES
Much better than average brewpub. Comfortable family restaurant/pub atmosphere. Growlers and kegs to go. Electronic dart board.

Elgin, Illinois
PRAIRIE ROCK BREWING COMPANY

127 South Grove, Elgin, IL 60120; phone 847-622-8888
Type: Brewpub
Near: Prairie Road, 1 block north of the Grand Victoria Riverboat Casino
Opens: 11:30 a.m. Monday-Saturday; noon Sunday
Prices: Average
Opening Date: October 1995
Most Popular Beer: Prairie Rock Ale and Honey Brown Ale
Brewing System: 15 barrel, Newlands Services

BEER LIST
••• **Prairie Rock Ale** (Golden Ale)–Cascade and Mt. Hood hops.
•• **Prairie Light** (American Light)
•• **Rockin' Red Ale**–Crystal malt sweetness with a mild hop finish.
••• **Honey Brown Ale**–Described by the brewery as "a medium bodied, dark malty brew with just a kiss of honey." A perfect description.
•• **Old Glory American Pale Ale**–Grapefruit-like cascade hop character.
   Prairie Porter
Seasonal Beers
•• **Vanilla Cream Ale**–Yep, it's a creamy vanilla ale. Reminiscent of an old fashion cream soda married with a light ale.
••• **Triple Nickel Irish Stout**–Served on nitrogen, producing a creamy head. A very nice dry stout.
• **Helmut's Dunkelweiss**–Unfiltered.
   I.P.A.
   Clock Tower Amber Lager

BREWERY NOTES
Above average brewpub. Known for their steak, ribs, and chops. Excellent, highly rated wine list. Located in a beautiful building that was once the Grove Theater. The theater opened in 1920 and closed for good in 1976. The restaurant has an expansive dining room and centrally located fireplace.

Flossmoor, Illinois
FLOSSMOOR STATION BREWING COMPANY

1035 Sterling Avenue, Flossmoor, IL 60422; phone 708-957-2739
E-mail: tashman@techinter.com
Type: Brewpub
Near: Flossmoor Road and Illinois Central railroad tracks
Nearby City: See Chicago
Opens: 11 a.m. Monday-Saturday; noon Sunday
Prices: Average
Opening Date: July 1996
Most Popular Beer: Station Master Wheat
Brewing System: 15 barrel, Specific Mechanical

BEER LIST

- •• **Station Master Wheat** (American Wheat)–Brewed with 50% wheat malt.
- • **Gandy Dancer** (Honey Ale)–A light ale with a subtle honey sweetness in the finish.
- •• **Zephyr Golden Ale**–Pacific Northwest hops. Light and refreshing.
- • **Chessie Cherry Wheat Ale**
- •• **Panama Limited Red**–Assertively hopped. Lingering citrus hop flavor.
- •• **Pullman Nut Brown**–Mellow and chocolaty.
- •• **Ironhorse Stout** (Oatmeal Stout)–Malty sweet, chocolaty, and smooth.
- • **Light Rail Amber**
- •• **Russian Imperial Stout**–Obvious alcohol kick in a rather smooth, malty, and roasty stout.

BREWERY NOTES

Converted historic 1906 train station. Nicely done, it offers a pleasant and unique family restaurant atmosphere. All beers lightly filtered. Model trains circle the bar on elevated tracks.

Glen Ellyn, Illinois
GLEN ELLYN BREWING COMPANY

433 North Main Street, Glen Ellyn, IL 60137; phone 630-942-1140
E-mail: gebcns@aol.com
Type: Brewpub
Near: Southeast corner of Main and Duane Streets, 1 block south of the
Metra train tracks
Nearby City: See Chicago
Opens: 11 a.m. daily
Prices: Average to expensive
Opening Date: June 1996
Most Popular Beer: Glen Ellyn Red
Brewing System: 10 barrel, New World Brewing System

BEER LIST
- **G.E. Light**
- **Glen Ellyn Red**
- **Hefe-Weizen**
- **Nut Brown Ale**
- **Mai-Bock**–Malty, with an obvious alcohol kick.
- **Milky Way Stout** (Milk Stout)–Surprisingly light bodied for a milk stout.
Nice roasty burnt malt character.

BREWERY NOTES
Housed in a 100-year-old brick building. American grill style restaurant. Attractive glassed-in brewery displayed in the dining area. Constantly rotates beers; over 20 different styles. The light, red, and stout are always available. Their beers can be found on tap in the surrounding area.

Lake Barrington, Illinois
WILD ONION BREWING COMPANY

28W039 Commercial Avenue, Lake Barrington, IL 53001
Phone: 847-304-1183
E-mail: wonion@juno.com
Web Address: www.wildonionbrewery.com
Type: Microbrewery
Near: Route 14 and 59 in an industrial park.
Nearby City: See Chicago
Open: 8 a.m.-6 p.m. Monday-Friday; 10 a.m.-2 p.m. Saturday
Opening Date: May 1997
Most Popular Beer: Paddy Pale Ale
Brewing System: 15 barrel, customized dairy tanks

BEER LIST
- ••• **Paddy Pale Ale**–Their only bottled beer as of 1998. The rest are available on various tap accounts. Northern Brewer, Cascade and Styrian Goldings hops.
- ••• **Bevo Brown Ale**–Named after a very friendly black Lab that hangs out at the brewery.

Seasonals:
Olde Ale
Pumpkin Ale
Berry Wheat
Wailin' Wheat

BREWERY NOTES
Wild Onion has several tap accounts, including "The Maproom" in Chicago, and locally at "Chessies," a converted train station in downtown Barrington. All their beers are bottle conditioned. Tours are available.

Why the name "wild onion?" The brewery takes its name from the origins of Chicago. When the first settlers arrived in the 1600s, wild onions grew along the banks of the Chicago River, and Indians called the area *Checagou*–wild onion!

Libertyville, Illinois
MICKEY FINN'S BREWERY

412 North Milwaukee Avenue, Libertyville, IL 60048
Phone: 847-362-6688
Web Address: www.mickeyfinnsbrewery.com

Type: Brewpub
Near: West Church Street
Nearby City: See Chicago
Opens: 11 a.m. Monday-Saturday; noon Sunday
Prices: Average
Opening Date: August 1994
Most Popular Beer: Wheat Ale and Five Springs Oatmeal Stout
Brewing System: 10 barrel

BEER LIST

- •• **Wheat Ale**–Brewed with 50% wheat malt. Mildly phenolic and slightly sweet.
- • **Raz** (Raspberry Wheat)
- •• **Güdendark Dunkel-Weizen**–Darker version of their hefe-weizen. Unfiltered, with good clove and banana character.
- ••• **Gasthaus Pils**–Medium bodied and mildly sweet pils. Clear straw golden, with a lightly salty and fresh hop finish.
- ••• **Five Springs Oatmeal Stout**–Sour and roasty. Silky smooth, served traditional Irish-style. On cask the sourness increases both in aroma and flavor, with an exceptionally silky body and suggestions of licorice.
- • **Oktoberfest**
- •••• **Abana Amber Ale**–Dry and spicy. Excellent on cask, it takes on a refreshing citrus character.
- •••• **Güdenteit Hefe-Weizen**–Strong fruity and spicy notes in medium bodied beer. Over 60% wheat malt.
  Güdenkrisp Kolsch

BREWERY NOTES

An excellent brewpub, with a friendly and comfortable atmosphere. Their ales are available cask conditioned, served in 20 ounce British pub glasses. I highly recommend trying them.

Lincolnshire, Illinois
FLATLANDERS BREWING COMPANY

200 Village Green, Lincolnshire, IL 60069; phone 847-821-1234
E-mail: rawbrew@aol.com
Type: Brewpub
Near: Milwaukee and Old Half Day Road (north of route 22)
Nearby City: See Chicago
Opens: 11 a.m. Monday-Friday; noon Saturday; 3:30 p.m. Sunday
Prices: Expensive
Opening Date: April 1996

BEER LIST
- **Harvest Amber**
- **Old Orchard Ale**–Brewed with wheat and red cherries.
- •• **Prairie Wheat** (American Wheat)
- ••• **Pilsner**
- **Oktoberfest**
- ••• **Locomotive Stout**–Jet black with ruby highlights. Roasty aroma and flavor. Hints of coffee and chocolate in the finish. Smooth mouthfeel.
- **80 Shilling**–Strongly smoky, more akin to liquid smoke than peat-smoked malts.
- •• **Abe's Honest Ale** (American-style Pale Ale)–Dry hopped. Assertive hop aroma and flavor. Thin bodied.

BREWERY NOTES
Classic Midwestern menu, lots of meat dishes. They even offer an ostrich burger. Gorgeous, spacious timber-frame building with an enormous off-center fireplace. Six-packs and growlers to go.

19

Moline, Illinois
BENT RIVER BREWING COMPANY

1413 Fifth Avenue, Moline, IL 61265
Phone: 309-797-2722, or toll free 888-797-BENT
E-mail: darronm@aol.com
Web Address: www.bentriverbrew.com
Near: 15th Street in the heart of downtown Moline, one block north of the Mississippi River.
Type: Microbrewery
Opens: 3 p.m. Monday-Thursday; 11 a.m. Friday; 3 p.m. Saturday; 5 p.m. Sunday
Opening Date: Winter 1998
Brewing System: 15 barrel

BEER LIST
   Bohemian Pilsner
   Premium Lager
   Amber Lager
   American Pale Ale
   Bavarian Weissbier
   Stout

BREWERY NOTES
Located in a 100-year-old historic building.

Naperville, Illinois
TAYLOR BREWING COMPANY

200 East Fifth Avenue, Naperville, IL 60563; phone 630-717-8000
Type: Brewpub
Near: Washington Street. Located in the 5th Avenue Station Mall, next to the Naperville train station.
Nearby City: See Chicago
Opens: 11:15 a.m. Monday-Saturday; noon Sunday
Prices: Average
Opening Date: January 1994
Most Popular Beer: Pilsner
Brewing System: 7 barrel

BEER LIST
Ales:
- **Palpitatious Porter**
- ••• **Prime I.P.A.**–Assertively hopped American-style I.P.A., with most of the hop character evident in the citrusy finish. Not highly bitter.
- ••• **Very Pale Ale** (Blonde Ale)–Great character in an American light ale. Nice citrusy hop finish.
- **Weizen**
- •• **Nut Brown Ale** (British-style)

Lagers:
    Equinox Lager
- •• **Golden Diamond** (American Lager)
- **Pure Pilsner**
- **Dark Satin** (German Dunkel)
    Maibock
    Sunset Amber

BREWERY NOTES
Rated as a "Top Ten Hamburger Restaurant" by the *Chicago Sun-Times*.

Peoria, Illinois
CROOKED WATERS BREWING

330 South West Constitution Avenue, Peoria, IL 61602
Phone: 309-673-2739
Web Address: www.crookedwaters.com
Type: Brewpub
Near: Harrison Street
Opens: 11 a.m. Monday-Saturday; noon Sunday
Prices: Average
Opening Date: 1996
Most Popular Beer: Powerhouse Amber Ale
Brewing System: 10 barrel, Specific Mechanical

BEER LIST

Waterfront Wheat (American Wheat)–Unfiltered.
Rivercity Razz (American Wheat with Raspberry)
Powerhouse Amber Ale (American-style Pale Ale)–Cascade hops.
Paddle Wheel Pale Ale (Golden Ale)
Steamboat Oatmeal Stout
Black & Tan–Oatmeal Stout and Powerhouse Amber Ale or Paddle Wheel Pale Ale.

Rock Island, Illinois
BLUE CAT BREW PUB

113 18th Street, Rock Island, IL 61201; phone 309-788-8247
Web Address: www.bluecatbrewpub.com
Type: Brewpub
Near: One half block from Illinois Route 92 and the Casino Rock Island. Two blocks from the Plaza One Hotel.
Opens: 11 a.m. Monday-Saturday; 3 p.m. Sunday
Opening Date: March 1994
Most Popular Beer: Off the Rail Pale Ale
Brewing System: 7 barrel, Newlands and Specific Mechanical

BEERS
Arkham Stout
Finnigan's Irish Stout
Bow Fish Imperial Stout
Blue Cat Porter
Gunther Bock
Audrey's Brown Ale
Crescent Moon E.S.B.
Wee Bit Scotch Ale
River Back Jack I.P.A.
Off the Rail Pale Ale
Pumpkin Ale
Cranberry Ale
Washington's Cherry Ale
Weiss Bock
Munich Helles
Scotch Terrier Rauchbier (smoked beer)

BREWERY NOTES
Located in a late 19th century building in the heart of downtown Rock Island, now called "The District." In 1993, the company began the restoration of this two-story brick building that spans half a city block. There are two different atmospheres available, one in the downstairs dining room and the other in the upstairs pub and pool hall.

South Barrington, Illinois
MILLROSE BREWING COMPANY

45 South Barrington Road, South Barrington, IL 60010
Phone: 847-382-7673
Type: Brewpub
Near: Corner of Barrington Road and Central
Nearby City: See Chicago
Opens: 11 a.m. Monday-Saturday; 10 a.m. Sunday
Prices: Average to Expensive
Opening Date: 1991
Most Popular Beers: Wheat-n-Honey Ale and Country Inn Ale
Brewing System: 7 barrel, Pub Brewing Company

BEER LIST
- •• **Country Inn Ale** (Blonde Ale)–A good light ale offering.
- ••• **Dark Star Lager** (American Dark Lager)–Malty with a moderate hop finish.
- •• **Prairie Pilsner**–Dry and lingering hop finish.
- •• **Panther Amber** (Strong Amber Ale)–A very nice amber, medium bodied with a caramel malt character.
  Wheat-n-Honey Ale
  General's Ale (American-style Pale Ale)–Northern Brewer and Cascade hops.
  WR Stout (Dry Stout)

BREWERY NOTES
A lavish country restaurant with timber-frame construction, exposed ceiling, wood paneling, carpeting and hardwood floors. The brewery is attached to the Millrose Country Store. A beer garden, with outdoor fireplaces, is also available. They received an award from the Chicago Beer Society for their Wheat-n-Honey Ale.

Villa Park, Illinois
LUNAR BREWING COMPANY

54 East St. Charles Road; Villa Park, IL 60181; phone 630-530-2077
Type: Brewpub
Near: Route 83
Nearby City: See Chicago
Opens: Noon daily
Opening Date: September 1997
Most Popular Beer: Raspberry Cream Ale
Brewing System: 3 barrel

BEER LIST & BREWERY NOTES
Too many beers to list. By brewing small batches they are able to rotate through up to 50 beers a year.

Warrenville, Illinois
TWO BROTHERS BREWING COMPANY

30W 114 Butterfield Road, Warrenville, IL 60555
Phone: 630-393-4800
E-mail: info@TheBrewersCoop.com
Web Address: www.twobrosbrew.com
Type: Microbrewery
Near: Route 59
Nearby City: See Chicago
Opens: Noon Tuesday-Friday; 10 a.m. Saturday; noon Sunday; closed Monday
Opening Date: March 1997
Most Popular Beer: Ebelweiss Wheat
Brewing System: 17.5 barrel

BEER LIST
••• **Brothers Best Brown**–Mild and slightly malty. A good introduction to a dark ale.
 • **Prairie Path Ale**
 • **Ebelweiss Wheat** (Bavarian-style Wheat)
   Monarch
   Wit
   Iditarod Imperial Stout–7.25% ABV

BREWERY NOTES
Tours are offered on the first Saturday of each month at 2 p.m. Growlers, six-packs, and kegs to go.

Westmont, Illinois
WEINKELLER BREWPUB

651 North Westmont Drive, Westmont, IL 60559
Phone: 630-789-2236
Type: Brewpub
Near: Ogden Street
Nearby City: See Chicago
Opens: 11 a.m. Monday-Saturday; 3 p.m. Sunday
Prices: Expensive
Opening Date: March 1992
Most Popular Beer: Bavarian Weiss
Brewing System: 15 barrel, Pub Brewing Company

BEER LIST

- ••• **Bavarian Weiss**–Cloudy, strong banana nose and flavor mixed with light clove. Very smooth, with a lightly sour finish.
- •• **Kristall Weiss**–Filtered. Less intensely flavored than the hefe-weizen.
- • **Berliner Weiss**–Unfortunately it is only available with raspberry syrup, obscuring much of the sour lactic character. Although this is an acceptable way to serve a Berliner-style weiss beer, it would be nice to have the option to try it unadulterated.
- •• **Pilsner**
- •••• **Aberdeen Amber Ale**–Complexly malty, with a nice caramel character. Excellent bitter finish.
- •••• **Nut Brown Ale**–Wonderfully mellow malty character. Light chocolaty finish. Delicious.
- ••• **E.S.B.**–Very good British ale character.
- •••• **I.P.A.**–Aggressively hopped, medium bodied I.P.A. Wonderful lingering hop bitterness, balanced by a strong malt body. Chinook, Fuggles, and Cascade hops.
- • **Bagpipe Scotch Ale**
- • **Marzen**
- •• **Dublin Stout**
- • **Duesseldorfer Doppelbock**
- •• **Maibock**

BREWERY NOTES

Primarily German cuisine. Weinkeller brews over 30 varieties of beers over the year, with over 12 beers on tap at any one time. All beers are brewed in accordance with the Reinheitsgebot purity law. Incredible bottled beer list, with over 150 beers from all over the world. Their bottled beer is available locally.

The original Weinkeller brewery, located in Berwyn, Illinois, was damaged by fire. As of August 1999, the future of that brewery was still uncertain.

BREWERIES OF INDIANA

INDIANA "BEST OF GREAT LAKES" BREWERIES
Lafayette Brewing Company (page 37)
Three Floyds Brewing Company (page 33)

ADDITIONAL RECOMMENDED INDIANA BREWERIES
Alcatraz Brewing Company (page 34)
Bloomington Brewing Company (page 29)

Bloomington, Indiana
UPLAND BREWING COMPANY

350 West 11th Street, Bloomington, IN 47404; phone 812-336-BEER
E-mail: upland@bluemarble.net
Web Address: www.uplandbeer.com
Type: Microbrewery and Restaurant
Near: Downtown Bloomington, Morton and 11th Street
Opens: 11 a.m. daily
Opening Date: April 1998
Most Popular Beer: Wit beer, Pale Ale, and Porter
Brewing System: 30 barrel, Northern Brewing Systems

BEER LIST
   Belgian Wit Beer
   American Amber
   American Pale
   Bad Elmer's Porter

BREWERY NOTES
Nestled in the uplands of southern Indiana, in downtown Bloomington (home of Indiana University). The brewery houses a bar and restaurant serving entrees, deli-style sandwiches, vegetarian fare and wines. Beers are sold throughout Indiana in bottles and kegs. Tours are available.

Bloomington, Indiana
BLOOMINGTON BREWING COMPANY

1795 East 10th Street, Bloomington, IN 47408; phone 812-323-2112
E-mail: bbc@bloomington.com
Web Address: bbc.bloomington.com
Type: Brewpub
Near: Between Fee and Union streets. Attached to Lennie's Restaurant and across the street from the Teter Dormitory.
Opens: 11 a.m. daily
Prices: Average
Opening Date: December 1994
Most Popular Beer: Quarrymen Pale Ale
Brewing System: 15 barrel, Specific Mechanical

BEER LIST
- ••• **Freestone Blonde**–Nice character in a blonde.
- •• **Vision Weiss**
- •• **American Wheat**–Strong wheat character.
- • **Ruby Bloom Amber**
- ••• **Quarrymen Pale Ale**–Excellent American-style pale ale.
- ••• **Big Stone Stout**–Roasty, with chocolate malt and smoky components.
- • **Highlander** (Scottish Heavy Ale)–Spring seasonal. Light with a slight smokiness.

BREWERY NOTES
One beer engine with rotating beers. All unfiltered beers. Southern Indiana's first microbrewery. Cozy pub and restaurant atmosphere. Clearly above average. Located near Indiana University, very involved with local and student charity events.

29

Evansville, Indiana
FIRKIN BREWPUB

329 Main Street, Evansville, IN 47708; phone 812-422-9700
Type: Brewpub
Near: 4th and Locust. Take Highway 41 to Walnut toward downtown,
   right on 4th
Opens: 11 a.m. daily; closed Sunday
Prices: Average
Opening Date: 1996
Most Popular Beer: Honey Blonde
Brewing System: 19 barrel

BEER LIST
- •• **Honey Blonde**–Over 60 pounds of clover honey in every batch.
- • **Firkin Gold**
- • **Brickstreet Amber**
- • **London Porter**
- •• **Yorkshire Stout**

BREWERY NOTES
English pub theme; however, unlike an English pub, their beers are served
very cold. Live bands.

Evansville, Indiana
MAIN STREET BREWERY

408 North Main Street, Evansville, IN 47711; phone 812-424-9871
Type: Brewpub
Near: Virginia Street
Opens: 11 a.m. weekdays; noon Saturday; 4 p.m. Sunday
Prices: Average
Opening Date: July 1996
Most Popular Beer: Turoni's Light Ale
Brewing System: 9 barrel

BEER LIST
- • **Turoni's Light Ale**
- • **Turoni's Ale**
- • **Thunderbolt Red Ale**
- • **Big Buck Pale Ale**
- • **Ol' 23 Stout** (Oatmeal Stout)–Named after Evansville native Don
  Mattingly.

BREWERY NOTES
Family restaurant atmosphere. The evening I visited, entertainment was provided by a wandering accordion player.

Fort Wayne, Indiana
MAD ANTHONY'S BREWING

2002 Broadway, Fort Wayne, IN 46802; phone 219-426-2537
Type: Brewpub
Near: Corner of Broadway and Taylor
Opens: 11 a.m. daily
Prices: Inexpensive
Opening Date: February 1998
Most Popular Beer: Old Fort Porter
Brewing System: 7 barrel

BEER LIST
- •• **Gabby Blonde**–Nice grainy blonde.
- • **Pan Head Red** (Amber Ale)
- • **Ol' Woody Pale Ale**–American-style pale ale with Cascade hops.
- ••• **Big Daddy Brown**–Light caramel flavor, with a chocolate malt finish.
   Old Fort Porter

BREWERY NOTES
Attached to the Munchy Emporium, a restaurant that pre-dates the brewery. Eclectic menu (voted Fort Wayne's best pizza). Great domestic and imported bottled beer selection. Growlers to go.

Greenwood, Indiana
OAKEN BARREL BREWING COMPANY

750 East Main Street, Greenwood, IN 46143; phone 317-887-2287
E-mail: obbc@oakenbarrel.com
Web Address: www.oakenbarrel.com
Type: Brewpub
Near: I-65 to the Greenwood Exit (exit 99), west 3/4 mile to the Vista Village complex (look for the building with the plane in the roof). Next to One Liners Comedy Club.
Nearby City: See Indianapolis
Opens: 11:30 a.m. weekdays; noon Saturday; closed Sunday
Prices: Average
Opening Date: July 1994
Most Popular Beer: Razz-Wheat
Brewing System: 7 barrel

BEER LIST
- **Big Red** (Amber Ale)
- **Snake Pit Porter**
••• **Razz Wheat**–A good fruit beer, strong raspberry flavor.
  King Rudi (Hefeweizen)
  Pale Ale–Chinook, Cascade, and Fuggles hops.
  Meridian Street Lager (Helles)
  Leroy Brown (Brown Ale)

BREWERY NOTES
"Nouveau American" cuisine. Specialty beers have included a Belgian-style tripel and dandelion mead. Oaken Barrel beer is available at a growing number of restaurants and bars throughout central Indiana. Accounts include the Slippery Noodle Inn (downtown), Grindstone Charley's (southside), and the Blue Heron (northside). Bottled beer is distributed around the Indianapolis area.

Hammond, Indiana
THREE FLOYDS BREWING COMPANY

6119 Calumet Ave, Hammond, IN 46320
Phone: 219-931-2537
Type: Microbrewery
Opening Date: 1996
Most Popular Beer: Alpha King
Brewing System: 5 barrel, Horeca

BEER LIST

•••• **Alpha King** (Pale Ale)–An excellent pale ale. Brewed with lot's of C's: Cascade, Chinook, Centennial, and Columbus.

•••• **X-tra Pale Ale**–Wonderfully resinous hop aroma and flavor. Moderately bitter finish that builds on the palate. Excellent.

•••• **Rabid Rabbit** (Saison)–A style of Belgian ale rarely brewed in the states. Unfiltered, nearly opaque, burnt orange color. Two varieties of Belgian yeast are employed to produce an unmistakably Belgian fruity complexity, present both in a powerful aroma and flavor. The addition of coriander contributes to its spicy, dry finish. An excellent and flavorful example of the style.

Pride & Joy (American Mild Ale)
Drunk Monk (Hefe-Weizen)
Robert the Bruce (Scottish Ale)
Black Sun Stout (Irish Dry Stout)
Behemoth Blonde Barley Wine

BREWERY NOTES

As of summer 1999, only the Alpha King and X-tra Pale Ale were available bottled; the rest of their beers are offered on draft in various locations. Unfortunately, the brewery does not offer any direct retail sales, but happily their bottled beers are now available outside of Indiana. Look for their draft beers locally and at the wonderful taproom in Chicago, the Maproom *(www.maproom.com)*.

The name "Three Floyds" is appropriate; the brewery was founded by Nick Floyd, his father, and his brother.

Indianapolis, Indiana

For Indianapolis breweries, also see Greenwood.

Indianapolis, Indiana
ALCATRAZ BREWING COMPANY

49 West Maryland, Indianapolis, IN 46204; phone 317-488-1230
Web Address: www.calcafe.com/alcatraz
Type: Brewpub
Near: Corner of Illinois and Maryland, near Planet Hollywood, adjacent to the United Artists Cineplex
Opens: 11 a.m. daily
Prices: Average
Opening Date: October 1995
Most Popular Beer: Big House Red

BEER LIST
- ••• **Searchlight Golden Ale**–An excellent blonde ale, strong grainy flavor and assertive hop finish.
- • **Weiss Guy Wheat** (American Wheat)
- •• **Big House Red**–Good caramel malt character.
- •••• **Dark Wheat Ale**–A wonderful synergy of coffee, roasted malt, and chocolate flavors. Finishing with wheat sourness and a hoppy finish. Excellent.
- •• **Breakout Stout**–Quite roasty, with a strong burnt malt character.
- • **First Degree E.S.B.**
  Racer "X" Rye
  Penitentiary Porter

BREWERY NOTES
Alcatraz Brewing is located in the touristy heart of downtown Indianapolis. Predictably there is a strong Alcatraz and San Francisco area motif, including a freestanding bar supported by replicas of the Golden Gate Bridge Towers. The décor is full of whimsical prison themes, and their motto is "best beers behind bars."

Other Alcatraz breweries are located in Auburn Hills, Michigan; Tempe, Arizona; and Denver, Colorado. Strange that there isn't one in San Francisco.

Indianapolis, Indiana
BROAD RIPPLE BREWING COMPANY

840 East 65th Street, Indianapolis, IN 46220; phone 317-253-2739
Type: Brewpub
Near: College Street
Opens: 11 a.m. daily
Prices: Average
Opening Date: 1990
Most Popular Beer: E.S.B.
Brewing System: 7 barrel, Century

BEER LIST
  Wheat–Varies seasonally between German and American style.
•• **E.S.B.**–Nicely hopped, with a good caramel malt nose and flavor.
•• **I.P.A.**–Styled after an English I.P.A. Aggressively hopped.
•• **Porter**–Caramel and chocolate overtones.
  Red Bird Mild
  Wee Alec Heavy (Scottish Ale)
  Lawnmower Pale Ale

BREWERY NOTES
A remodeled home with the brewpub sign mounted on an old basketball pole. Homey pub atmosphere. Two beer engines serving cask conditioned beer. Live blues every Sunday.

Indianapolis, Indiana
CIRCLE V BREWING COMPANY

8310 Craig Street, Indianapolis, IN 46250; phone 317-595-9253
Type: Brewpub
Near: 82nd Street
Opens: 11:30 a.m. daily
Prices: Inexpensive
Opening Date: April 1996
Most Popular Beer: Brickyard Red Ale
Brewing System: 15 barrel, Criveller

BEER LIST
 • **Craig Street Wheat**
•• **Venus Blonde**
 • **Brickyard Red Ale**
•• **Bullseye Bitter** (English Bitter)
 • **Muddy Waters Brown Ale**
•• **Pacer Pale Ale**–Dry hopped
  Probate Porter

BREWERY NOTES
Knowledgeable waitstaff. Ranked the #2 brewpub in Indianapolis in October 1997 issue of *Nuvo*.

Indianapolis, Indiana
ROCK BOTTOM BREWERY #9

10 West Washington Street, Indianapolis, IN 46204; phone 317-681-8180
Web Address: www.rockbottom.com
Type: Brewpub
Near: Washington and Meridian
Opens: 11 a.m. weekdays; noon Saturday and Sunday
Prices: Average to expensive
Opening Date: June 1996
Most Popular Beer: Sugar Creek Pale Ale
Brewing System: 12 barrel, J.V. Northwest

BEER LIST
  Sugar Creek Pale Ale
  Indianapolis Golden Ale
  Wagon Train Wheat (American Wheat)
  Raccoon Red
  Brickway Brown (American Brown)
  Hoosier Ma (Oatmeal Stout)–7% ABV

BREWERY NOTES
Large Colorado based brewpub chain with many locations. Twelve or more
specialty beers every year that vary seasonally. Generally 7 to 8 beers on tap
at anyone time.

Indianapolis, Indiana
WILDCAT BREWING COMPANY

9111 North Michigan Road, Indianapolis, IN 46260; phone 317-872-3446
Type: Brewpub
Near: 86th Street
Opens: 11 a.m. daily
Prices: Expensive
Opening Date: 1997
Most Popular Beer: Lion's Eye Red Ale and Pridelands Wheat Ale

BEER LIST
  • **Roaring Raspberry Ale**
  • **Sabre Tooth Stout**
  Spotted Leopard Light (Light Beer, 90 calories)
  Panting Panther Pale Ale
  Lion's Eye Red Ale
  Pridelands Wheat Ale (Bavarian Style)
  Cheetah Cherry Wheat
  Predator Porter

BREWERY NOTES
Cat theme.

Lafayette, Indiana
LAFAYETTE BREWING COMPANY

622 Main Street, Lafayette, IN 47901; phone 765-742-2591
E-mail: lbrewco@dcwi.com
Type: Brewpub
Near: 2 Blocks East of Tippecanoe County Courthouse
Opens: 11 a.m. daily; closed Sunday
Prices: Average
Opening Date: September 1993
Most Popular Beer: Black Angus Oatmeal Stout
Brewing System: 7 barrel, Century Manufacturing

BEER LIST
Flagship Beers:
•••• **Prophet's Rock Pale Ale**–An easy drinking American pale ale. Brewed with Cascade hops which provides its somewhat muted citrusy quality. Finishes with a touch of crystal malt sweetness.
••• **Black Angus Oatmeal Stout**–Brewed with five malts, 10% oatmeal, and Northwest hops. Silky smooth, with a sweet finish and mild roastiness.
•••• **White Tail Wheat** (American Wheat)–Cloudy, nearly incandescent, golden colored ale. Brewed with 50% wheat malt, and Northwest hops. Soft and somewhat sour, possessing much more character than is typical in the style. Quite quenching.
•••• **East Side Bitter** (E.S.B.)–An outstanding English-style bitter. It's available either on tap or cask conditioned; I recommend the cask version. Brewed with English hops and caramel malts, this beer captures the often-elusive essence of an English cask-conditioned bitter. A deep copper colored beer, rich in caramel-like maltiness, with a silky smooth body. The hops provide a skillful balance, not terribly overt initially, with a bitterness that gradually builds as the pint empties.
Seasonal Beers:
•••• **Weeping Hog IPA**–Styrian Goldings, Willamette, and Challenger hops. Smooth, with a great bitter finish. Terrific on cask.
•••• **Digby's Irish Stout**–Mellow, with a wonderful chocolate malt character and black licorice-like finish. Absolutely delicious.
•••• **Plaza Extra Pale Ale**–Mellow and wonderful on cask.
•••• **2 Penny Wee Mild** (Scottish Ale)

(continued)

Lafayette Brewing Company (cont.)

•••• **Old No. 85** (I.P.A.)–This beer derives its name from its whopping 85 IBU's (International Bitterness Units. A typical pale ale has IBU numbers in the 20-40 range). As one would expect, this beer is quite bitter. It exhibits some citrus-like character, which is quickly overwhelmed by a powerful finishing bitterness that actually continues to build. For those who enjoy a very hoppy beer, as I do, this one is pure bliss.

•• **Heritage Trail Amber Ale**
Big Boris Barleywine
Smokehouse Porter–Peat smoked pale malts.
Piper's Pride Scotch Ale–Peated Scotch ale.
Third Eye Rye
Summer Solstice Kolsch
Christmas Ale

BREWERY NOTES

While all the beers at Lafayette Brewing are good, all unfiltered and served at the proper temperature, their outstanding cask-conditioned ales set them apart. Each cask-conditioned beer is served via English beer engine. My advice for choosing a beer here is to simply find out what's on cask that day and order it.

Lafayette Brewing Company is located in a turn-of-the-century brick building in Lafayette's historic downtown shopping district. The brewpub has been locally owned and operated since inception. The brewery's philosophy emphasizes traditional ale styles, while the restaurant serves hearty, freshly prepared meals in a casual atmosphere.

LaPorte, Indiana
BACK ROAD BREWERY

1315 Michigan Avenue, LaPorte, IN 46350; phone 219-324-9251
Type: Microbrewery
Near: Corner of Lake and Tyler streets
Open: Tours 1-4 p.m. Saturday
Opening Date: April 1997
Most Popular Beers: BackRoad Ale and Millennium Lager
Brewing System: 7 barrel

BEER LIST
BackRoad Ale–Flagship beer.
Millennium Lager
Blueberry Ale
Summer Wheat (American Wheat)
Belle Guinness Stout–Named after an infamous LaPorte native.
Midwest I.P.A.–American hops.
Christmas Ale
Autumn Ale

BREWERY NOTES
Bottled beer available all over northwest Indiana and on tap at Rosco's in
LaPorte.

Michigan City, Indiana
DUNELAND BREWHOUSE

5718 South Franklin, Michigan City, IN 46360; phone 219-878-9180
Type: Brewpub
Near: 400 yards north of I-94 on Franklin Street, which is Route 421
Opens: 11 a.m. daily
Prices: Average to Expensive
Opening Date: June 1997
Most Popular Beer: Salmon Tail Pale Ale
Brewing System: 15 barrel, Specific Mechanical

BEER LIST
- **Lighthouse Light** (Pilsner)
- **Open Hearth Amber Ale**
- **Bubba's Brown**
- **Salmon Tail Pale Ale**–Cascade hops.
- **Shoreline Stout**–Very light stout.
- **Hefe-Weizen**
  Raspberry Wheat
  I.P.A.–Fuggles hops

BREWERY NOTES
Family restaurant atmosphere. Growlers to go.

Mishawaka, Indiana
MISHAWAKA BREWING COMPANY

3703 North Main Street, Mishawaka, IN 46545
Phone: 219-256-9994 (brewery); 219-256-9993 (restaurant)
E-mail: misbrew@aol.com
Type: Microbrewery and Restaurant
Near: Edison Street
Opens: 11:30 a.m. Monday-Saturday; noon Sunday
Prices: Average
Opening Date: October 1992
Most Popular Beer: Four Horsemen Ale
Brewing System: 8½ barrel, Specific Mechanical

BEER LIST
- **Mishawaka Gold Lager**
- **Raspberry Wheat**
- **Wall Street Wheat** (American Wheat)
- •• **Dominator Doppelbock**–8.3% ABV.
- ••• **Founder's Stout** (Irish Dry Stout)–Brewed with seven varieties of malt. Smooth and roasty, with coffee and bittersweet chocolate notes.
- ••• **Lake Effect Pale Ale**–A blend of Mt. Hood, Willamette, and Cascade hops. Light bodied and citrusy.
- •• **INDIAna Pale Ale** (I.P.A.)–Bigger bodied than their pale ale, exhibiting good complexity from 5 varieties of hops.
- •• **Four Horsemen Ale** (E.S.B.)–Hints of toffee in a caramel malt body. Slightly buttery mouthfeel.
- **German Alt Beer**

BREWERY NOTES
Near South Bend. Pool tables and darts are available in a sports bar/family restaurant atmosphere. They generally offer approximately 8 beers on tap, with growlers, 22-ounce "bombers," and 12-ounce bottles to go.

Salem, Indiana
TUCHER BREWING COMPANY

1477 South State Road 60, Salem, IN 47167; phone 812-883-4393
Email: nd90@blueriver.net
Type: Microbrewery
Near: Salem's only stoplight
Opens: 9 a.m. Monday-Saturday; closed Sunday
Opening Date: July 1995
Most Popular Beer: Blackberry Wheat and Salem Ale
Brewing System: 7 barrel, Elliott Bay

BEER LIST
Salem Ale (I.P.A.)–Fuggles and East Kent Golding hops.
Blackberry Wheat
Brown Ale
Smoked Porter

BREWERY NOTES
Beer available for sale, small samples provided. Distributed in Indiana and Kentucky. Rural setting. Beer can museum.

BREWERIES OF MICHIGAN

MICHIGAN "BEST OF GREAT LAKES" BREWERIES

Arbor Brewing Company (page 44)
Arcadia Brewing Company (page 48)
Dragonmead Microbrewery (page 98)
Kalamazoo Brewing Company (page 72)
Michigan Brewing Company (page 100)
New Holland Brewing Company (page 67)
North Channel Brewing Company (page 52)
Rochester Mills Beer Company (page 90)
Roffey Brewing Company (page 68)

ADDITIONAL RECOMMENDED MICHIGAN BREWERIES

Atwater Block Brewing (page 54)
Big Rock Chop and Brew House (page 49)
Bob's House of Brews (page 64)
Boyne River Brewing Company (page 50)
Copper Canyon Brewery (page 93)
Dark Horse Brewing Company (page 80)
Detroit Brew Factory (page 58)
Jackson Brewing Company (page 70)
Kraftbräu Brewery (page 74)
Lake Superior Brewing Company (page 63)
Lighthouse Brewing Company (page 78)
Local Color Brewing Company (page 83)
Motor City Brewing Works (page 55)
Olde Peninsula Brewpub and Restaurant (page 75)
Royal Oak Brewery (page 91)
Traffic Jam and Snug (page 56)
Traverse Brewing Company (page 102)

Ann Arbor, Michigan
ARBOR BREWING COMPANY

114 East Washington, Ann Arbor, MI 48104
Phone: 734-213-1393
E-mail: info@arborbrewing.com
Web Address: www.arborbrewing.com
Type: Brewpub
Near: Main Street
Opens: 11:30 a.m. Monday-Saturday; noon Sunday
Prices: Average
Opening Date: July 1995
Most Popular Beer: Big Ben House Mild and Terminator Doppelbock
Brewing System: 7 barrel, DME

BEER LIST
Year Round:
•••• **Big Ben House Mild** (Golden Ale)–Very light bodied and mildly sweet, with a delicate yet lingering hop balance. A remarkably quaffable and quenching light ale.
•••• **Red Snapper Special Bitter**–An outstanding hybrid of English and American-style pale ales. Assertively hopped, including dry-hopping, this beer exhibits an excellent toasted malt character that adds appreciably to its complexity. It makes a wonderful and unique black and tan when combined with the Irish Stout.
•••• **Cask Conditioned I.P.A.**–Bitter, with strong citrus overtones. Dry hopping provides for a powerful hop nose. A great American I.P.A. served at cellar temperature.
•••• **Faricy-Fest Irish Stout**–Rich and creamy with a complex roasted barley character, hints of bittersweet chocolate, coffee, and a subtle smokiness.
•••• **Cask Conditioned Milestone Porter**–Light carbonation results in a wonderfully silky mouthfeel. An exceptionally rich and complex beer: mellow, roasty, slightly sour, chocolaty, and malty sweet. Brewed with 6 varieties of malt.
Seasonals:
••• **Olde No. 22 German Alt**–Nice initial malty character, with hints of chocolate. The finish is somewhat hoppy. An easy drinking dark ale.
•••• **No Parking Pilsner**–Imported German hops give this beer a magnificent nose and a dry, salty finish. Modeled after the classic Jever Pilsner of Germany.

Arbor Brewing Company (cont.)

•••• **The Jackhammer Old Ale**–Malty and complex. Fruity character reminiscent of chocolate covered cherries. Strong alcohol component. 8.5% ABV.

•••• **Bavarian Bliss Wheat Beer** (Bavarian-style Wheat)–A cloudy golden, served in traditional glassware. Clove-like spiciness combined with light wheat sourness. Very refreshing.

••• **Uskratsch Mai Bock**–Spicy and malty with a dry finish. Sound out the name of this one for a laugh; of course, it gets even funnier after you drink a few.

••• **80 Shilling Scottish Ale**–Smoky with a light malt body. Cask conditioned and served at cellar temperature.

•••• **Fat Abbot Belgian Tripel**–Sweet, with a distinctly Belgian fruitiness and dry spicy finish. Brewed with Belgian candi sugar. 8.5% ABV.

•••• **Oktoberfestbier**–Fall colored reddish-orange beer. Spicy hop character competes for attention with a strong malt body. Certainly one of the finest American brewed Oktoberfest beers I have sampled.

•••• **Terminator Doppelbock**–Somewhat of a legend in Ann Arbor, this is an eagerly awaited beer to aid in the fight against the bitterly cold Michigan winters. Each year they fabricate a new (and graphically violent) tap handle to celebrate its release in the beginning of December. A bloody axe, a morning star, and a guillotine have been previous years' tap handles. Big bodied and malty, with a caramel-like nose and flavor. Finishes spicy and dry. Go easy on this one; the Terminator isn't just a clever name. 9% ABV.

•••• **Steamroller Imperial Stout**–A wickedly potent brew. Served via hand-pull, at cellar temperature, this beer is dangerously easy drinking. Its huge alcoholic nose warns of the 11% ABV that will follow. The Steamroller is a malty beer up front, with caramel and bitter chocolate notes, as well as the expected fruity complexities of the style. The finish is somewhat bitter.

BREWERY NOTES

Offering wonderful beer and food, Arbor Brewing is one of the finest brewpubs in the Great Lakes region and is a must-visit for anyone traveling anywhere near Ann Arbor. Their unfiltered beers are served in traditional glassware and at the proper temperature, in a homey, warm and comfortable, European-style pub setting. Two cask-conditioned ales are served via traditional English beer engines. Their menu features classic pub fare plus many innovative vegetarian options.

Beer tastings are offered the second Thursday of each month. Each tasting focuses on a different style of beer, with numerous domestic and imported examples. The $20 per person admission price includes a buffet. Arbor Brewing is also very involved with local charity events, including a regularly scheduled homeless breakfast.

Ann Arbor, Michigan
GRIZZLY PEAK BREWING COMPANY

120 West Washington Street, Ann Arbor, MI 48104; phone 734-741-7325
Type: Brewpub
Near: Main Street
Opens: 11 a.m. Monday-Saturday; noon Sunday
Prices: Average
Opening Date: August 1995
Most Popular Beer: Steel Head Red
Brewing System: 7 barrel, Peter Austin

BEER LIST
- •• **Victor's Golden Ale**–Fresh, grainy and light, with a clearly perceptible hop contribution.
- ••• **Grizzly Peak Pale Ale**–Refreshing grapefruit-like hop finish from 100% Cascade hops. Nice American-style pale ale.
- • **Steel Head Red**
- •• **Cask Conditioned E.S.B.**–Acceptable interpretation of an English-style ale. Smooth with a clear alcohol aroma and flavor.
- ••• **Bear Paw Porter**–Roasty, slightly sour, and smooth. Suggestions of chocolate. A bit drier and roastier than the norm, definitely pint-worthy.
- •• **County Cork's Irish Stout**–Smooth, dry and roasty. On a nitrogen tap.

BREWERY NOTES
Fairly standard American brewpub atmosphere. Attractive red-brick walls. Lots of Grizzly Peak wearables and collectibles are available for sale.

Ann Arbor, Michigan
LEOPOLD BROS. OF ANN ARBOR

529 S. Main Street, Ann Arbor, MI 48104; phone 734-747-9806
Type: Microbrewery & Taproom
Near: Packard and Madison streets
Opening Date: Scheduled to open fall 1999
Brewing System: 20 barrel, DME

BREWERY NOTES
They plan to brew all German-style lagers, with all organic ingredients. The brewery is designed to recover and reuse all the waste heat generated in the brewing process, along with several other strategies to maximize efficiency. Reportedly they will be the first zero-waste brewery in the world.

Auburn Hills, Michigan
ALCATRAZ BREWING COMPANY

4362 Baldwin Road, Auburn Hills, MI 48326; phone 248-745-3400
Type: Brewpub
Near: Located in the Great Lakes Crossing Mall, near the District 6 entrance
Nearby City: See Pontiac.
Opens: 11 a.m. daily
Opening Date: November 1998
Brewing System: 15 barrel

BEER LIST
- •• **Searchlight Golden Ale** (Blonde Ale)–Flavorful training wheels beer.
- •• **Weiss Guy Wheat**–Light malt body, a touch of sourness, and a very light hop finish. A delicate American wheat.
- • **Big House Red**
- ••• **Birdman Brown Ale**–Nutty and mildly sweet.
- ••• **Lights Out Stout** (Irish Dry Stout)–Light to medium bodied. Finishes dry and lightly roasty.

BREWERY NOTES
At the time of my visit, this Alcatraz location had only been open for about a month, and their beers were not yet at the same level of quality as the Indianapolis location. They seemed lighter and more watery.

Other Alcatraz breweries are located in Indianapolis; Tempe, Arizona; and Denver. (Strange that there isn't one in San Francisco.) Predictably, there is a strong Alcatraz and San Francisco area motif. The décor is full of whimsical prison themes, and their motto is "best beers behind bars."

Auburn Hills, Michigan
BIG BUCK BREWERY AND STEAKHOUSE

2550 Takata Drive, Auburn Hills, MI 48326; phone 248-276-2337
E-mail: pres@bigbuck.com
Web Address: www.bigbuck.com
Type: Brewpub
Nearby City: See Pontiac
Opens: 11 a.m. daily
Prices: Average to expensive
Opening Date: September 1997
Most Popular Beer: Buck Naked Light and Big Buck Beer
Brewing System: 7.5 barrel, JV Northwest

BEER LIST AND BREWERY NOTES
See Gaylord Big Buck Brewery.

47

Battle Creek, Michigan
ARCADIA BREWING COMPANY

103 West Michigan Avenue, Battle Creek, MI 49017
Phone: 616-963-9520
E-mail: tsurprise@aol.com
Type: Microbrewery and Restaurant
Near: Kellogg's World Headquarters
Opens: 11 a.m. weekdays; noon Saturday; closed Sunday
Opening Date: October 1996
Most Popular Beer: Arcadia I.P.A.
Brewing System: 25 barrel, Peter Austin

BEER LIST
Year Round:
- •• **Battle Creek Special Reserve**–Entry-level beer.
- •• **Angler's Ale**–Their flagship ale.
- ••• **Lake Superior ESB**–Good bottled, and great on cask at the brewery.
- ••• **Nut Brown Ale**–Hints of chocolate, mildly sweet and easy drinking.
- ••• **Starboard Stout**–Oat malt stout, Northwest American hops. Smooth, roasty and chocolaty with a light bitterness.
- •••• **India Pale Ale**–Possibly the best I.P.A. brewed in the Midwest. Very assertively hopped, yielding incredible hop complexity, including a resinous pine needle character. The bitter finish lingers and gradually builds.

Seasonals:
- •••• **Olde Smoked Porter**–Very strong, full-bodied, and nearly black porter. Thick foamy head, rich chocolaty malt body, and a lingering bitter finish. Complex, with additional flavors of alcohol, ripe fruit, coffee, hints of caramel, molasses and a subtle smokiness.
- ••• **Autumn Ale**–Complex and spicy beer.
- •••• **Arcadia Whitsun**–"A modern interpretation of a mid-19th century English spring and summer festival ale." It is one of the finest honey-wheat beers I have sampled. Unfiltered and cloudy-golden with a clearly detectable but not overpowering honey flavor. 6% ABV.

BREWERY NOTES
British ale house. Note that their I.P.A. is their best seller. It's unusual for a best-selling beer to be something other than the lightest; nice to see that trend broken from time to time. Always two cask-conditioned ales available. Known for their wood-fired pizza. Live music and two pool tables.

Berkley, Michigan
O'MARA'S RESTAURANT AND BREWPUB

2555 Twelve Mile Road, Berkley, MI 48072; phone 248-399-6750
Type: Brewpub
Nearby City: See Detroit
Brewing System: 2 barrel

BEER LIST
Pilsner
American Lager
Amber Wheat
Ale
Triple Bock
Hearty Stout

Birmingham, Michigan
BIG ROCK CHOP AND BREW HOUSE

245 South Eton Street, Birmingham, MI 48009; phone 248-647-7774
Type: Brewpub
Near: 15 Mile Road
Nearby City: See Detroit.
Opens: 11 a.m. Monday-Saturday; 3 p.m. Sunday
Prices: Expensive
Opening Date: August 1997
Most Popular Beer: Norm's Raggedy Ass Ale
Brewing System: 15 barrel, DME

BEER LIST
•• **Norm's Raggedy Ass Ale**–Somewhat fruity, with a nice bitter finish.
• **Raymondo El Rojo**–A rather buttery red ale.
•• **Flying Buffalo Stout** (Oatmeal Stout)–Silky smooth and sour with a big chocolate and roasty bitter finish.
•• **Weizenheimer Hefe-Weizen**–Brewed with 60% malted wheat.
••• **Oktoberfest**–Copper colored. Malty with spicy accents.
••• **Belgian Wit**

BREWERY NOTES
Upscale and visually interesting brewpub (a huge flying buffalo hangs from the ceiling) with a colorful and unique decor. I'd call it whimsically Native American, with a heavy buffalo motif. The brewery refers to it as a Montana hunting lodge decor. Whatever it is called, Big Rock is certainly worth a look. No expense has been spared. In addition to the main dining area, they offer a martini and cigar lounge, complete with cask-conditioned ales via hand pull. Formerly the Eton Street Station Restaurant.

Boyne City, Michigan
BOYNE RIVER BREWING COMPANY

419 East Main Street, Boyne City, MI 49712; phone 616-582-5588
E-mail: hilly@triton.net
Web Address: www.boyneriver.com
Type: Microbrewery and Restaurant
Near: Corner of Boyne Avenue and Main Street
Opens: 11:30 a.m. Monday-Saturday; noon Sunday
Prices: Inexpensive to average
Opening Date: July 1995
Most Popular Beer: Lake Trout Stout
Brewing System: 7 barrel, Hilly System

BEER LIST

10:30 Ale (Golden Ale)–Named after the Boyne City fire whistle that sounds each night.

Hefe-Weizen–67% malted wheat, bottle conditioned.

Log Jam Ale (Special Bitter)

• **Nit Wit Ale** (Belgian Wit)

••• **Pale Ale**–Light bodied and very drinkable hoppy ale. Citrusy hop character, nice lingering bitter finish.

Brown Ale

Pumpkin Ale

••• **Lake Trout Stout**–Medium to full bodied with an agreeable combination of roasted malt and hop bitterness; hints of chocolate and fruit.

Oatmeal Stout

BREWERY NOTES

Nestled in a small resort town in northern Lower Michigan. A great place to visit for a leisurely, inexpensive lunch or dinner, in a remarkably cozy small-town pub atmosphere. All their beers for distribution are bottle conditioned, and they make an excellent root beer, "Hannah's Rootbeer," named after the owner's daughter.

Clinton Township, Michigan
GREAT BARABOO BREWING COMPANY

35905 Utica Road, Clinton Township, MI 48035; phone 810-79-BREWS
Type: Brewpub
Near: North corner of Utica Road and Moravian
Nearby City: See Detroit
Opens: 11 a.m. Monday-Saturday; 10:30 a.m. Sunday
Prices: Expensive
Opening Date: July 1995
Most Popular Beer: Kings Peak Caribou Brew Wheat and Sharks Tooth
  Bay Golden Ale
Brewing System: 7 barrel, DME

BEER LIST
- •• **Kings Peak Caribou Wheat** (American Wheat)–Unfiltered, 30% wheat malt.
- • **Snake Eye Canyon Red Ale**
- • **Sharks Tooth Bay Golden Ale**–Light, cold, and heavily carbonated.
- • **Boston Blackstone Porter**

BREWERY NOTES
First brewpub in the Macomb country area. All beers are served quite cold.
Mug Club membership for $25 provides many discounts and entitlements.
Ten-foot big screen TV for sporting events.

Chesterfield, Michigan
NORTH CHANNEL BREWING COMPANY

30400 23 Mile Road, Chesterfield, MI 48047
Phone: 810-948-BEER

Type: Brewpub
Near: ½ mile east of I-94
Opens: 11 a.m. Monday-Saturday; noon Sunday
Prices: Expensive
Opening Date: August 1998
Most Popular Beer: Whitetail Wheat
Brewing System: 15 barrel, Specific Mechanical

BEER LIST
St. Clair Light (Helles)
Whitetail Wheat

•••• **Harsen's Hefe-Weizen**–Excellent. Cloudy, with strong clove and banana character, along with clear wheat sourness. Very refreshing and flavorful.

•••• **Redhead Rye**–Brewed with malted rye, which supplies a unique spiciness in this rather light bodied, copper colored ale. Finishes spicy, hoppy, and dry.

•••• **Anchor Bay Pale Ale** (American-style Pale Ale)–The brewery describes this one as having "an explosion of hops." They aren't kidding! Intensely citrus-like hop burst, reminiscent of biting into a grapefruit, with a resinous hop character. Lightly bodied and clean, it's all about the hops.

•••• **The Great Pumpkin Ale**–Much better than average pumpkin ale. Dry, spicy nose accurately forecasts this spicy, light-bodied slice of pie in a glass. 5% ABV.

••• **Frostbite**–A spiced winter beer. Seven different malts, cranberries, honey and almonds are used to make this interesting, complex, and intensely spiced winter seasonal.

BREWERY NOTES
This brewpub does an excellent job of brewing "true-to-style" beers, while simultaneously giving their beers a unique character of their own. They also offer at least one new beer every week.

(continued)

North Channel Brewing Company (cont.)

North Channel has a somewhat upscale fishing and hunting decor, with lots of stuffed animals, mounted fish and the like. Sandwich selection includes a Buffalo burger. Entrees include fish and chips, perch, walleye, salmon, roast duck, ribs, and steak. A "Brewmaster's Dinner" is offered once a month, pairing several beers with a multi-course meal.

A selection of cigars is available. Cigar and pipe smoking is limited to the bar, which has an attractive view of the glassed-in brewhouse.

Commerce Township, Michigan
CJ'S BREWING COMPANY

8115 Richardson Road, Commerce Township, MI 48382
Phone: 248-366-7979
Type: Brewpub
Near: Haggerty Road
Opens: 11 a.m. Monday-Saturday; noon Sunday
Prices: Expensive
Opening Date: December 1997
Most Popular Beer: CJ's Gold
Brewing System: 7 barrel

BEER LIST
CJ's Gold
American Wheat
Lower Strait Stout
Rich Hagg Red Ale
Vat 33 India Pale Ale

BREWERY NOTES
Southwest of the Pontiac area. Usually six or more beers on tap.

Detroit, Michigan

For Detroit breweries, also see these nearby cities: Berkley, Birmingham, Clinton Township, Eastpointe, Ferndale, Rochester, Royal Oak, Southfield, Warren, Westland, Wyandotte

Detroit, Michigan
ATWATER BLOCK BREWING

237 Joseph Campau, Detroit, MI 48207; phone 313-393-2337
E-mail: beerisgood@sprynet.com
Type: Microbrewery and Restaurant
Near: 1 mile east of the Renaissance Center in downtown Detroit
Opens: 11 a.m. Monday-Friday; noon Saturday and Sunday
Prices: Average to expensive
Opening Date: March 1997
Most Popular Beer: Dunkel
Brewing System: 25 barrel

BEER LIST
Year Round:
>   Atwater Rost
•••• **Kräusen Hell**–Grainy and fresh malt aroma and flavor. Crisp mouthfeel, soft malt sweetness, lightly hopped. Very refreshing.
•• **Kräusen Dunkel**–Lightly malty. Hints of chocolate in the finish.
••• **Atwater Pilsner**–Crystal clear pils, well attenuated, not very bitter, with a lightly salty hop finish.
Seasonals:
••• **Dunkel Weizen**–Unfiltered. Nice phenolic clove and banana characteristics.
>   **Atwater Big League Brew**–A beer brewed to be served at Tiger Stadium.
••• **Atwater Winter Bock**–Light-to-medium copper color. Some caramel malt flavor. Finishes slightly spicy. 6.8% ABV.
•••• **Atwater Hefe-Weizen**–Excellent Bavarian-style wheat.
• **Atwater Kolsch**

BREWERY NOTES
Located in Detroit's Rivertown district, occupying a refurbished 1916 factory building. Features a state-of-the-art German brewing system and an upscale restaurant. Atwater focuses on German style ales and lagers and uses ingredients imported from Germany.

Beer to go in six-packs, growlers, and kegs. Brewery tours every Saturday at 1:30 p.m. and 2:30 p.m. A variety of fine cigars and Atwater Block merchandise is available.

Detroit, Michigan
MOTOR CITY BREWING WORKS

470 West Canfield Street; Detroit, MI 48201; phone 313-832-2700
E-mail: mcbw@mich.com
Web Address: www.motorcitybeer.com
Type: Microbrewery
Near: South of Wayne State University
Open: Variable hours
Opening Date: January 1995
Brewing System: Custom system

BEER LIST
- **Pale Ale**
- •• **Ghettoblaster**–Patterned after an English Mild. Medium amber color. Caramel malt sweetness with virtually no hop contribution.
- •• **Nut Brown Ale**
- •••• **Honey Porter**–A very dark and roasty porter. Flavorful chocolaty malt body, with a rather subtle honey contribution. Nicely balanced. Check out the wonderfully surreal bottle label.

BREWERY NOTES
Located in Detroit's historic Cass Corridor, the first new Detroit brewery since prohibition. Sells beer to go.

Each year the brewery releases the "Ghettoblaster Compilation CD," featuring some of Detroit's most original musical talent and recorded in their own studio. See their web page for ordering information.

Detroit, Michigan
TRAFFIC JAM AND SNUG

511 West Canfield, Detroit, MI 48201; phone 313-831-9470
E-mail: tjsnug@mich.com
Web Address: www.traffic-jam.com
Type: Brewpub
Near: Wayne State University
Opens: 11 a.m. Monday-Friday; 5 p.m. Saturday; closed Sunday
Prices: Average to expensive
Opening Date: December 1992
Most Popular Beer: Java Porter
Brewing System: 10 barrel

BEER LIST
- ••• **Nut Brown Ale**–Mild, dry, nutty character, somewhat malty, with a light suggestion of chocolate in the finish.
- •• **India Pale Ale**–Thin bodied for an I.P.A., but finishes decidedly bitter.
- •••• **Java Porter**–Dark and creamy. Medium bodied and malty, with a long-lasting rich chocolate and coffee finish.

BREWERY NOTES
Michigan's first brewpub. Traffic Jam and Snug offers a warm and comfortable décor and phenomenal food. Their beers are above average and all unfiltered. Over 100 bottled wines to choose from. Their large, eclectic menu includes "baked wild rice and cashew stuffed acorn squash," which is fantastic. Traffic Jam and Snug evolved from a beer and burger bar in 1965. Their name was inspired by a lack of parking. The brewery is noteworthy for sharing space with a dairy that produces many varieties of cheese and ice cream.

East Lansing, Michigan
HARPER'S RESTAURANT AND BREWPUB

131 Albert Street, East Lansing, MI 48823; phone 517-333-4040
Type: Brewpub
Near: Abbott Road across from Michigan State University
Opens: 11 a.m. daily
Prices: Expensive
Opening Date: Fall 1997
Most Popular Beer: Harper's Light
Brewing System: 15 barrel, DME

BEER LIST
- •• **Amber Ale**–Malty with a spicy dry finish.
- •• **Harper's Light**–Good training-wheels beer.
- •• **American Wheat**–Unfiltered and lightly sour.
- •• **Pale Ale**–Lightly citrusy American pale.
- •• **Weizen Bock**–Unfiltered. Brewed with honey, which provides a distinctive sweetness. Clear phenolic characteristics.
- •• **Sweet Stout**

BREWERY NOTES
Dance club downstairs called "Down-Town," formerly known as "Sensations." Big screen TV behind an attractive bar. Pool tables.

RECOMMENDED BREWERY

Eastpointe, Michigan
DETROIT BREW FACTORY

18065 East 8 Mile, Eastpointe, MI 48021; phone 810-776-8848
Type: Microbrewery and Taproom/Brew-on-Premise
Near: West of I-94, across from Eastland Mall
Nearby City: See Detroit
Open: Variable hours; call first
Opening Date: January 1997
Most Popular Beer: Centennial Ale
Brewing System: 1 barrel

BEER LIST
Nut Brown Ale
••• **Pigskin Porter**–Malty and chocolaty, with a satisfying finish that includes a lingering hoppiness.
Stanley Red Ale
••• **Michigan Lakes I.P.A.**–Reminiscent of a British-style ale. Rather light bodied, a bit caramel-like. Assertive bitter finish that lingers and grows.
•••• **Centennial Ale** (I.P.A.)–Dark copper color, foamy light amber head. The hoppy nose accurately predicts a potent hop bitterness and flavor. This hoppiness is nicely complimented with a toasty, complex malt character.
••• **Great Lakes Ale**–Amber colored, apparently unfiltered. Flowery, thin bodied, finishing slightly dry.
•••• **English E.S.B.**–Excellent British aroma and palate. Medium bodied with a clear caramel-like malt sweetness, and a proper bitter finish. It successfully put me in mind of a British pub–well done!
Caesar's Red Ale
• **Smoked Scotch Ale**
•• **Rye in Your Eye Ale**

BREWERY NOTES
A very nice, cozy little taproom with six beers on tap at all times. Their bottled beer is available to go, in singles, six-packs, mixed packs, and growlers. Over 75 different recipes to choose from if you would like to brew your own beer.

Escanaba, Michigan
HEREFORD & HOPS

624 Ludington Street; Escanaba, MI 49829; phone 906-789-1945
E-mail: hereford_hops@uplogon.com
Web Address: www.visit-usa.com/mi/delta/brewpub.htm
Type: Brewpub
Opens: 11 a.m. Monday-Saturday; 4 p.m. Sunday
Prices: Average
Opening Date: December 1994
Brewing System: 7 barrel

BEER LIST
- **Wolverine Wheat Beer**
  Pintail Pils
- **Whitetail Ale**
- **Cleary Red**
- **Steelhead Stout**
- **I.P.A.**

BREWERY NOTES
In Michigan's Upper Peninsula. Five house beers are always available.

Ferndale, Michigan
WOODWARD AVENUE BREWERS

22646 Woodward Avenue, Ferndale, MI 48826; phone 248-546-3696
E-mail: GJBrew@aol.com
Type: Microbrewery and Restaurant
Near: One block south of Nine Mile on east side of Woodward Avenue
Nearby City: See Detroit
Opens: 11 a.m. Monday-Saturday; noon Sunday
Prices: Average
Opening Date: May 1997
Most Popular Beer: Custom Blonde
Brewing System: 15 barrel, DME

BEER LIST
Year Round:
- **Custom Blonde**
- **Raspberry Blonde**
- **Custom Bronze** (Amber Ale)
- **Pale Ale**
- •• **Brown Ale**–Nutty and lightly malty.
- •• **Custom Porter**–Hints of chocolate with a hoppy finish. My favorite of the bunch.
  Vanilla Porter
Seasonals:
  Hefe-Weizen
  Oktoberfest
- •• **Pumpkin Ale**–Spiced with nutmeg, mace, and clove.
  Stout

BREWERY NOTES
The first restaurant in Ferndale to offer a summer sidewalk café. Deli-style menu includes some entrees prepared with their house beer. Homemade root beer and cream soda are also available. A pool table and various pinball and arcade games are provided for entertainment, as well as occasional live music. The brewery has tentative plans to begin bottling sometime in 1999.

Flint, Michigan
REDWOOD LODGE
MESQUITE GRILL AND BREWPUB

5304 Gateway Center, Flint, MI 48507; phone 810-233-8000
E-mail: redwood@voyager.net
Type: Brewpub
Near: US-23 and I-75 in the Gateway Center near the Holidome
Opens: 11 a.m daily
Prices: Expensive
Opening Date: December 1997
Most Popular Beer: Lucky LaRue's All American Lager
Brewing System: 15 barrel, DME

BEER LIST
- **Lucky LaRue's All American Lager**
- **Copper Mountain Märzen**
- **Redwood Local Ale** (Mild Ale)
- **Burke's Best Brown Ale**–Very tasty. Described as a "free style brown," probably more of an American porter. Rather sweet, with a strong chocolate malty character and coffee roastiness. My favorite of the bunch.
- **Space Stout** (Dry Stout)
- **Nut Brown Ale**
  Rooftop I.P.A.

BREWERY NOTES
To my knowledge they are the only brewery in the region brewing all their beers with certified organic ingredients, a praiseworthy effort. The brewer is known as the "Organic Mechanic." At least one cask conditioned ale is always available.

Gorgeous, lavish lodge atmosphere. Offerings include wood fired pizzas, a very impressive bottled beer and wine list, and a cigar room with bar. Full line of merchandise.

Gaylord, Michigan
BIG BUCK BREWERY AND STEAKHOUSE

550 South Wisconsin, Gaylord, MI 49735; phone 517-732-5781
E-mail: pres@bigbuck.com
Web Address: www.bigbuck.com
Type: Microbrewery and Restaurant
Near: Exit 282 off I-75. Look for the giant beer bottle.
Opens: 11:30 a.m. daily
Prices: Average to Expensive
Opening Date: May 1995
Most Popular Beer: Buck Naked Light and Big Buck Beer
Brewing System: 20 barrel, J.V. Northwest

BEER LIST
> **Buck Naked Light** (American Light Lager)
> **Wolverine Wheat**
> •• **Big Buck Beer**
> **Raspberry Wheat**
> **Antler Ale**
> ••• **Redbird Ale**
> ••• **Doc's E.S.B.**
> ••• **Black River Stout**
> •• **Black'n Berry**–Unique "black and tan" twist. A combination of their stout and their raspberry wheat.

BREWERY NOTES
Massive, ornate northern lodge atmosphere. Northern hunting theme with plenty of stuffed wildlife. Huge beer bottle outside doubles as a grain silo.

Up to 16 beers on tap. Beer selections are divided into a "mainstream line" of light varieties, as well as a more robust and challenging line of beers. Six-packs to go.

See also the Big Buck Breweries in Grand Rapids and Auburn Hills.

Grand Marais, Michigan
LAKE SUPERIOR BREWING COMPANY

N-14283 Lake Avenue, P.O. Box 310, Grand Marais, MI 49839
Phone: 906-494-2337
Type: Brewpub
Opens: Noon daily
Prices: Average
Opening Date: August 1995
Most Popular Beer: Sandstone Pale Ale
Brewing System: 6 barrel

BEER LIST
- ••• **Sandstone Pale Ale** (American-style Pale Ale)–Dry hopped.
- • **Puddingstone Light** (American Wheat)
- • **Jasper Cherry** (American Wheat)
- ••• **Sandstone Light** (Blonde Ale)–Very light flavor, with a smooth and refreshing light citrus/hop finish.
- ••• **Granite Brown**–Nice brown ale. Mild and light bodied as the style calls for, with a light chocolaty malt finish.
- •• **Agate Amber**–Copper colored and cloudy. Moderately hopped and lacking a bit in body. Slightly metallic aftertaste.
- •• **Hematite Stout**–Medium bodied with a malty roastiness. Definitely on the sweet end of the spectrum.

BREWERY NOTES
Located near Pictured Rocks National Lakeshore on Lake Superior in Michigan's Upper Peninsula. Cozy "country store" atmosphere. Pool table, jukebox, pinball, and a very cool "Rock Museum" for entertainment. All beer is unfiltered.

Grand Rapids, Michigan
BIG BUCK BREWERY AND STEAKHOUSE

2500 28th Street SE, Grand Rapids, MI 49501; phone 616-954-9635
E-mail: pres@bigbuck.com
Web Address: www.bigbuck.com
Type: Microbrewery and Restaurant
Near: About 2 miles west of I-96 near Brenton Road
Opens: 11:30 a.m. daily
Prices: Average to Expensive
Opening Date: March 1997
Most Popular Beer: Buck Naked Light and Big Buck Beer
Brewing System: 15 barrel, J.V. Northwest

BEER LIST AND BREWERY NOTES
See Gaylord Big Buck Brewery.

Grand Rapids, Michigan
BOB'S HOUSE OF BREWS

20 Monroe Avenue NW, Grand Rapids, MI 49503; phone 616-356-2000
Web Address: www.thebob.com
Type: Brewpub
Near: Corner of Fulton and Monroe, across from the Van Andel Arena
Opens: 4 p.m. Monday-Friday; 11:30 a.m. Saturday; closed Sunday
Prices: Average
Opening Date: June 1997
Most Popular Beer: Festive Amber
Brewing System: 15 barrel, Pico

BEER LIST
   I.P.A.
   Bob's Saaz Pils
 •• **Festive Amber**–Thin, with a bit of a metallic zing in the finish.
   Smoky Scotch Ale (90 Shilling)
 ••• **Broommaster Stout**–Fairly big bodied. Silky, malty and roasty, with coffee-like notes.
 ••• **13 Malt Ale**–Unfiltered. Smooth mouthfeel, slightly sour.
 •• **Pilsner**–Hoppy with a lingering bitter finish. Saaz hops.
 •••• **Celtic**–Sweet and malty with hints of smoke. A few sips put me in mind of Scotland.
 •••• **Hoppy Holiday** (I.P.A.)–Dark amber color, and as the name suggests, aggressively hopped. Strong, with a clear alcohol component.

BREWERY NOTES
Above average beers and very good food. Located in the B.O.B. (Big Old Building), an entertainment complex of five restaurants, a pool hall, cigar lounge, wine cellar, mini theater, and comedy club. The brewery supplies beer for the entire complex.

Grand Rapids, Michigan
CANAL STREET BREWING COMPANY

648 Monroe NW, Grand Rapids, MI 49503; phone 616-776-1195
E-mail: founders@iserv.net
Web Address: www.foundersales.com
Type: Microbrewery and Taproom
Near: Monroe and Michigan
Opens: 5 p.m. Wednesday-Saturday
Opening Date: January 1998
Most Popular Beer: Founders Weizenbier
Brewing System: 30 barrel, Sprinkman

BEER LIST
- **Founders Pale Ale**
- **Founders Weizenbier**
- ••• **Founders Porter**–Roasty aroma, light-medium body. Finishes with an aggressive and lingering hop bitterness and flavor.
- **Founders Red Ale**

Grand Rapids, Michigan
GRAND RAPIDS BREWING COMPANY

3689 28th Street, Grand Rapids, MI 49512; phone 616-285-5970
Type: Brewpub
Opens: 11 a.m. daily
Prices: Average
Opening Date: 1993
Most Popular Beer: Silver Foam
Brewing System: 7 barrel, DME

BEER LIST
- **Silver Foam**
- **Fruit and Spice** (rotating fruit beer)–An orange blossom Hefe-Weizen when I sampled it.
- **River City Red**
- **Lumberman Dark** (Porter)
- **I.P.A.**
- •• **Rotating Sixth Tap**–An E.S.B. when I sampled it.

Grand Rapids, Michigan
ROBERT THOMAS BREWING COMPANY

2600 Patterson Avenue SE, Grand Rapids, MI 49546
Phone 616-942-6820
Type: Microbrewery and Taproom
Near: Corner of Star and Patterson streets
Opens: 5 p.m. Tuesday-Friday; noon Saturday; closed Sunday
Opening Date: 1998
Brewing System: 20 barrel

BEER LIST
- •• **Par 5 Pale Ale**–Light hoppy aroma, thin bodied.   Mild, yet satisfying, lingering bitter finish.
- • **Hefe-Weizen**
- ••• **King's Cross Porter**–Very dark and roasty with a rather assertive bitter finish. Chocolate malt sweetness.
- • **Four Seasons Amber**

BREWERY NOTES
Beers are also available on tap at the "Taps Sportsbar" near the Van Andel Arena.

Holland, Michigan
BACK STREET BREWING COMPANY

13 West 7th, Holland, MI 49423; phone 616-394-4200
Type: Brewpub
Near: Off I-196
Opens: 11:30 a.m. daily
Opening Date: 1998
Brewing System: 10 barrel

BREWERY NOTES
Formerly the Black River Bistro, a brewpub that closed after a short time of operation.

Holland, Michigan
NEW HOLLAND BREWING COMPANY

205 Fairbanks Avenue, Holland, MI 49423
Phone: 616-355-6422
E-mail: newholland@novagate.com
Web Address: www.newhollandbrew.com
Type: Microbrewery and Taproom
Near: Corner of Fairbanks and 8th
Open: 8:30 p.m. to midnight Tuesday-Wednesday; 4 p.m.-midnight
Thursday-Saturday; closed Sunday and Monday
Opening Date: July 1997
Most Popular Beer: Paleooza
Brewing System: 30 barrel, Sprinkman

BEER LIST

••• **Paleooza**–A fine American-style pale ale, nice yeasty fruitiness.

•••• **Zoomer Wit** (Belgian-style Wheat)–Great example of the style.

•••• **Mad Hatter**–At the brewery they refer to this one as an "insanely dry-hopped ale." Call me crazy, I love it. Strong citrus nose and an aggressive hop finish. A very tasty I.P.A.

•••• **Kourage** (Dark Ale)–Originally to be named Dutch Kourage, which means the courage acquired from drinking alcohol. It's a dark, medium-bodied ale, with a wonderfully hoppy nose and a big chocolate malt character. Finishes assertively hoppy.

••• **Olde Poet** (Oatmeal Stout)–Smooth, creamy and roasty. Moderately malty body.

•••• **Ichabod** (seasonal pumpkin ale)–Nutmeg up front with a pumpkin flavor that gradually merges with the spice. Dry spicy finish. 7% ABV.

•••• **Cabin Fever**–Their winter seasonal. A reddish-amber beer, brewed with rye. Very spicy, intensely hoppy, and yeasty. 6.5% ABV.

BREWERY NOTES
Great atmosphere in the taproom. Friendly staff. Very simple, low key, and utilitarian, it's all about the beer. An absolutely wonderful place to hang out and put down a few pints. Peanuts, popcorn, and beef jerky are available to soak up the beer, or you can order a pizza to be delivered. Pool tables and dart boards. Six-packs, cases, and half-barrels to go.

Holland, Michigan
ROFFEY BREWING COMPANY

697 Lincoln Avenue, Holland, MI 49423
Phone: 616-355-2739
E-mail: roffeybrewing@novagate.com

Type: Microbrewery
Near: 20th and Lincoln
Open: 8 a.m.-5 p.m. weekdays; 11 a.m.-3 p.m. Saturday; closed Sunday.
Opening Date: June 1996
Most Popular Beer: Forecaster Pale Ale
Brewing System: 14 barrel

BEER LIST
•••• **Wheat Wave Ale** (American Wheat)–Soft and perfumy hop nose. Lingering bitter hop finish. Crisp and refreshing. An excellent wheat.
•••• **Forecaster Pale Ale**–Medium bodied pale ale with a strong hop aroma, an aggressive resinous hop flavor, and moderate bitterness. Cascade and Centennial hops.
•••• **Lake Effect Stout**–Very dark, almost completely black, stout. Full-bodied with an intense black malt roastiness and a significant hop contribution. Lingering bitter finish. Hints of chocolate.

BREWERY NOTES
Brewery tours available. Beer for sale at the brewery in a variety of containers.

Houghton, Michigan
LIBRARY BAR AND RESTAURANT

62 North Isle Royale, Houghton, MI 49931; phone 906-487-5882
Type: Brewpub
Near: Downtown area
Opens: 11:30 a.m. Monday-Saturday; 5 p.m. Sunday
Opening Date: Started brewing October 1997
Most Popular Beer: Keweenaw Gold
Brewing System: 5 barrel

BREWERY NOTES
In Michigan's Upper Peninsula.

Ishpeming, Michigan
JASPER RIDGE BREWERY

1075 Country Lane, Ishpeming, MI 49849; phone 906-485-6017
Type: Brewpub
Near: ½ mile from the U.S. National Ski Hall of Fame.
Opens: 11 a.m. daily
Prices: Average
Opening Date: October 1996
Most Popular Beer: Ropes Golden Wheat
Brewing System: 10 barrel, Pico

BEER LIST
- **Ropes Golden Wheat** (American Wheat)–50% wheat malt. Offers up a bit of wheat sourness.
- **Red Earth Pale Ale**–Fairly assertive hop bite in the finish.
- **Jasper Brown Ale**–Light bodied and easily drinkable with a nice mellow maltiness. A bit too carbonated.
- **Kölsch**–Captures some of the character of the style.
  Jasper Lyte Lager
  Raspberry Wheat

BREWERY NOTES
In Michigan's Upper Peninsula. Sports bar atmosphere.

Jackson, Michigan
JACKSON BREWING COMPANY

6020 Ann Arbor Road, Jackson, MI 49201; phone 517-764-5010
Type: Brewpub
Near: Sargent Road, Exit 145 off I-94
Opens: 11 a.m. daily
Prices: Expensive
Opening Date: February 1996
Most Popular Beer: Cascade Gold
Brewing System: 15 barrel

BEER LIST
- •• **Cascade Gold**
- ••• **Puddleford Pale Ale**–Assertively bittered with imported English hops.
- ••• **Mad Jackson's Red** (California Common)–Toasted malt character provides a good accompaniment to the citrus-like American Pacific Coast hops.
- •••• **Crossroads Porter**–Brewed with a large variety of malts, complex and roasty. Silky mouthfeel, lightly carbonated. Very nice.
- ••• **St. James Gate Stout**–A good example of an Irish dry stout. Light bodied with a roasty palate. Thin and dry.
- •••• **Double Brown**–Dark amber color. Quite malty, with hints of ripe fruit. A very tasty and potent ale. 8% ABV.
- ••• **I.P.A.**–Strongly citrusy, grapefruit-like bitterness.

BREWERY NOTES
Easily accessible off I-94. Above average brewpub serving 20-ounce beers brewed in the British tradition. Upscale atmosphere. Dinner entrees include, prime rib, porterhouse, filet mignon, trout, lamb, duck, New York strip, salmon, baby back ribs. Most entrees over $15.

$35 to join their their mug club. Club members receive handmade mugs, 22 ounces or bigger, that can be filled for regular price. A variety of additional perks are available to members.

Kalamazoo, Michigan
BILBO'S PIZZA AND BREWING COMPANY

2628 West Michigan Avenue, Kalamazoo, MI 49008; phone 616-382-5544
Type: Brewpub
Near: Corner of West Michigan Avenue and Howard Street, near the
Western Michigan University campus
Opens: 11 a.m. daily
Prices: Average
Opening Date: Started brewing May 1998
Most Popular Beer: Wizard Wheat
Brewing System: 3 barrel

BEER LIST
    Wizard Wheat
    Dragon Red Ale
- **Underground Brown**
- **All American Pale Ale**
- **Honey Porter**

BREWERY NOTES
Tolkien Middle Earth theme. They plan to brew many different styles and seasonals. Voted best pizza in Kalamazoo several times. Specialty pizza doughs.

BELL'S

Kalamazoo, Michigan
KALAMAZOO BREWING COMPANY
355 East Kalamazoo Avenue, Kalamazoo, MI 49007
Phone: 616-382-2332
Web Address: www.bellsbeer.com

Type: Regional Brewery and Taproom
Opens: 10 a.m. daily; noon Sunday
Opening Date: 1985
Most Popular Beer: Bell's Amber
Brewing System: 15 and 30 barrel systems

BEER LIST
Flagship Beers:
- **Bell's Amber**–An outstanding and distinctive American amber ale. Alcohol and yeast aromas are evident. Malty and yeasty flavor, some ale fruitiness, and a wonderful spicy dry finish.
- **Bell's Pale Ale**–Golden color, slightly cloudy, with a soft fine white head. A complex and flowery nose, with strong yeast and caramel notes. Medium bodied, somewhat fruity and very yeasty palate, featuring an assertive hop character that lingers in a long finish.
- **Bell's Porter**–A surprisingly complex porter. Dark brown with a thick, rich, tan head. Slightly smoky palate mingles with a strong ale fruitiness and sweet chocolate malt finish.
- **Bell's Best Brown**–A great American brown ale. Dark amber colored and cloudy, with a yeasty, malty nose. Satisfying malt character balanced with a mildly bitter finish. A bit big for the style, but delicious.
- **Bell's Kalamazoo Stout**–No brewery anywhere makes stouts and other potent ales any better than the folks at Kalamazoo Brewing. For most breweries a stout like this would be their biggest beer, but at Bell's they are just getting started. Black with ruby hues and foamy tan head. A thick, rich and chewy body that's powerfully balanced by roasty malt bitterness and hops. Hints of molasses, chocolate and fruit. 6.5% ABV.
- **Third Coast Beer**–One of their lightest bottled beers. Perfumy and flowery hop nose, soft malt body. Yeasty flavor with a lightly resinous hop character. A flavorful, light-bodied pale ale.

Kalamazoo Brewing Company (cont.)

Seasonals:

•••• **Bell's Oberon** (American Wheat)–A classic American wheat, and a tasty thirst quencher. Extremely popular.

•••• **Two Hearted Ale** (I.P.A.)–A distinctive and intense I.P.A. bursting with heavy and resinous hop aroma and flavor. A "hop-head's" delight.

Bell's Special Double Cream Stout

•••• **Third Coast Old Ale** (Barley Wine)–A deep copper color with a sweet and hoppy nose. It is simultaneously both hoppy and richly malty, with an interesting complexity that includes a distinctive fruitiness. Although high in alcohol, it is remarkably drinkable. The label depicts a stark, cold winter scene; what a perfect beer for such a day. 10.2% ABV.

•••• **Bell's Expedition Stout** (Barley Wine) –Jet black, with virtually no head. This is a dark, rich, and robust beer, brewed with double the malt and 5 times the hops of the Kalamazoo Stout. After a few sips there is no mistaking the rather high (10% ABV) alcohol content conspicuous in aroma, flavor and comforting warmth. Somewhat masked is a soft, fruity character.

•••• **Java Stout**–A beer that will wake you up and put you down simultaneously. Richly malty with a strong coffee kick. Varies considerably from year to year.

•••• **Bell's Cherry Stout**–Michigan tart cherries married with a jet-black stout. This, like other Bell's beers, is in no way subtle. Tart cherry flavor dominates, nicely supported with a rich stout body.

•••• **Bell's Eccentric Ale** (Christmas Ale)–The brewery describes this one as "a monster of a beer"; I quite agree. It is brewed once a year and unveiled in December during a wonderful celebration called "Eccentric Day." The dominant flavor components are alcohol (11% ABV), and a staggering complexity of malt, hops, and spice. It is extraordinarily hopped, and spiced with ingredients such as juniper, coriander, caraway, and others. This beer is warming, filling, and extremely intoxicating. At $5 a bottle it's quite expensive, but worth it for anyone interested in trying a very distinctive holiday ale.

Bell's Harvest Ale
Bell's Sparkling Ale

BREWERY NOTES

Larry Bell started the brewery with a 15-gallon soup kettle in 1985. From those simple beginnings, Kalamazoo Brewing Company (known simply as "Bell's" throughout Michigan) has matured into one of the finest microbreweries in the country. It specializes in unfiltered, bottle-conditioned beers brewed with distinction and personality. More than a few beer lovers consider a trip to the brewery a pilgrimage.

The Eccentric Café, an attached taproom, opened in June 1993. Light snacks, great beer, and an eclectic variety of bands are offered. Call the brewery for information on live band schedules.

Brewery wearables, homebrew supplies, and more are available at the Bell's General Store.

Kalamazoo, Michigan
KRAFTBRÄU BREWERY

402 East Kalamazoo Avenue, Kalamazoo, MI 49007
Phone: 616-384-0288
Type: Microbrewery and Taproom
Near: Porter Street across from Kalamazoo Brewing Company
Opens: 4 p.m. daily; closed Sunday
Opening Date: September 1996
Brewing System: 6 barrel, customized dairy tanks

BEER LIST

- **Berliner Weiss**–Very light sourness, with no significant lactic character.
•••• **Helles**–Very fresh malt nose with a soft malty body. True German character. Easy drinking.
- **Vienna**
••• **Dunkel**–Hints of chocolate.
•••• **Altbier**–Dry hopped with Cascades. Nice hybrid of German malt and American hops.
  Pils
••• **Munich Red**–Tettnanger hops.
  Doppelbock

BREWERY NOTES

All German-style beers. Cozy and comfortable, simply decorated. Wonderful college pub atmosphere. Live bands. Inexpensive popcorn is available.

Kalamazoo, Michigan
OLDE PENINSULA BREWPUB
& RESTAURANT

200 East Michigan Avenue, Kalamazoo, MI 49007
Phone: 616-343-BREW
Type: Brewpub
Near: Downtown Kalamazoo, corner of Portage Road and Michigan Avenue
Opens: 11 a.m. daily; closed Sunday
Prices: Average
Opening Date: 1996
Most Popular Beer: Rockin' Raspberry Wheat
Brewing System: 7 barrel, DME

BEER LIST
- ••• **Haymarket Ale** (Wheat Ale)–Fresh grainy flavor and light hop finish.
- • **Sunset Red**–Perle and Hallertauer hops
- ••• **Rockin Raspberry Wheat**–Fresh raspberry nose. Has none of the artificial character prevalent in the style. One of the best I've had.
- ••• **Tornado Pale Ale**–Unfiltered. Refreshing light bodied pale ale with a rather strong bitter finish.
- •• **Midnight Stout**–Nice chocolate malt character with a smidgen of sourness and some black malt bitterness.
- •• **Black Raspberry**–A blend of the Rockin' Raspberry Wheat and Midnight Stout. Good, but I felt they were better separate.
- •• **Black and Tan**–Haymarket Ale combined with the Midnight Stout.
- •• **Pumpkin Ale**–Strong nutmeg spiciness.

BREWERY NOTES
Above average brewpub and Kalamazoo's first. The building once housed the Kalamazoo Stove Company, a bookbindery, and a hotel. Several unique dishes are made with their house beer.

Lansing, Michigan

For Lansing breweries, also see these nearby cities: East Lansing, Okemos.

Lansing, Michigan
BLUE COYOTE BREWING COMPANY

113 Pere Marquette, Lansing, MI 48912; phone 517-485-2583
Type: Brewpub
Near: Off Michigan Avenue near Cedar Street
Opens: 11 a.m. Monday-Saturday; 3 p.m. Sunday
Prices: Expensive
Opening Date: 1996
Most Popular Beer: I.P.A.
Brewing System: 15 barrel

BEER LIST
- **Woodsman Wheat** (American-style)–Unfiltered.
- **I.P.A.**–Citrusy but very light for an I.P.A.
- **2 River Red**
- **Raspberry Wheat**–Artificial tasting raspberry.
- **Capitol City Light**–Called "Lugnut Light" during baseball season, in reference to Lansing's minor league baseball team, the Lugnuts.

BREWERY NOTES
Stylishly renovated warehouse with worn hardwood floors, brick walls, and exposed wood ceilings. Wood-fired pizzas. Cigars available. Weekly live music.

Lansing, Michigan
LANSING BREWING COMPANY

1105 River Street, Lansing, MI 48912; phone 517-485-2739
Type: Microbrewery
Near: Cedar Street (U.S.-27 business route)
Opens: Variable hours
Opening Date: May 1997
Most Popular Beer: Timbermen's Blonde Lager
Brewing System: 10 barrel, Groen

BEER LIST
Year Round:
  Amber Cream Beer
  Timbermen's Blonde Lager
Seasonals:
  Centennial Stout
  Winterfest Ale
  Weiss-Pils–Equal parts pilsner and wheat malts. 100% Saaz hops and
  ale yeast. Outside of Belgium, I have not seen this style brewed.

BREWERY NOTES
Winner of the "People's Choice Award" for their Amber Cream Beer at the
1997 Michigan Festival.

The Lansing Brewing Company is unique. Unlike most other breweries,
they are not simply brewing American versions of traditional European styles.
Instead, they have tried to model many of their beers as variants on the California
Common beer style. Since these beers are not easily categorized, trying
to rate them would be too subjective. Instead, I will simply recommend
them to anyone interested in trying a uniquely American beer.

The original Lansing Brewing Company was located in the city's Old Town
business district and successfully operated until 1913, when a Local Option
was adopted by the citizenry, effectively rendering Lansing a dry city until
1933.

Lawton, Michigan
OLD HAT BREWING

114 North Main Street, Lawton, MI 49065; phone 616-624-6445
Type: Microbrewery and Taproom
Near: Located in downtown Lawton
Opens: 4 p.m. Monday, Wednesday and Friday; noon Saturday-Sunday; closed Tuesday
Opening Date: October 1998
Most Popular Beer: Kölsch and Hefe-Weizen
Brewing System: 7 barrel, Specific Mechanical

BEER LIST
Alt
Kölsch
Hefe-Weizen
Vienna
Doppelbock

BREWERY NOTES
Featuring all German-style beers. Peanuts and some other snack foods available. Same ownership as Kalamazoo Brewing Company.

Manistee, Michigan
LIGHTHOUSE BREWING COMPANY

312 River Street, Manistee, MI 49660; phone 616-398-2739
Type: Microbrewery and Restaurant
Near: West of Highway 31
Opens: 11 a.m. Tuesday-Saturday; noon Sunday; closed Monday
Prices: Expensive
Opening Date: November 1998
Most Popular Beer: Golden Ale
Brewing System: 40 barrel, fully automated DME

BEER LIST
•• **Amber Ale**–3 varieties of hops. Lightly spicy finish.
••• **Pale Ale**–Medium bodied and citrusy, assertive bitter finish.
••• **Golden Ale** (Kölsch)–Lightly fruity, with a subtle hop finish.
•• **Brown Ale** (American Brown)–A bit too carbonated.

BREWERY NOTES
Named for the Manistee lighthouse. A somewhat upscale restaurant atmosphere with a banquet room and elegant dining available upstairs. Gorgeous old building with original red brick walls and a huge glassed-in brewery. It dates back to 1895 and used to be the Elks Lodge.

The brewery plans to distribute upwards of 70 percent of beer production in Michigan and Ohio. Wines for in-house consumption will be produced at an on-site winery. They also produce their own handcrafted root beer, cream soda and sarsaparilla soda.

Marquette, Michigan
VIERLING RESTAURANT &
MARQUETTE HARBOR BREWERY

119 South Front Street, Marquette, MI 49855; phone 906-228-3533
E-mail: brewman21@aol.com
Type: Brewpub
Near: Corner of Front and Main streets in downtown Marquette
Opens: 11 a.m. daily; closed Sunday
Prices: Average
Opening Date: October 1995
Most Popular Beer: Landlooker Honey Wheat
Brewing System: 5 barrel, Bohemian Brewery Importers

BEER LIST
- • **Amos Harlow's Amber Ale**
- • **Landlooker Honey Wheat**
- •• **Captain Ripley's Red Ale**–Nicely balanced.
- ••• **Spear's Tug Stout**–Served on nitrogen, it has a creamy head and body. A very roasty, malty, and chocolaty nose accurately predicts the flavor. Significantly sweeter than Guinness, this beer is closer to Murphy's Irish Stout. A commendably flavorful and complex stout, clearly the best of the bunch.
- •• **Plank Road Pale Ale**–Extremely strong citrusy hop flavor, supported by a slightly malty body.
  Traverse City Cherry Wheat
  Peter White Peach Wheat
  Main Street Brown Ale
  Canadian Blonde Ale
  1919 Rootbeer

BREWERY NOTES
In Michigan's Upper Peninsula. Housed in a wonderful red brick building that used to be the Vierling Saloon back in 1883. Lovely view of Lake Superior off the dining room. Selected as "Best Restaurant" by *Marquette Magazine*.

Marshall, Michigan
DARK HORSE BREWING COMPANY

826 West Michigan, Marshall, MI 49068; phone 616-781-7797
E-mail: sparkfish@aol.com
Type: Brewpub
Near: Old 27 and Michigan Avenue near the Brooks Memorial Fountain.
Opens: 11 a.m. daily; closed Sunday
Prices: Average
Opening Date: October 1997
Most Popular Beer: Historic Krystal Wheat and Special Reserve Black Bier
Brewing System: 7 barrel

BEER LIST
- ••• **Historic Krystal Wheat**
- ••• **Big Al's Cranberry Wheat**–Unfiltered wheat ale flavored with real cranberries that provide a distinctly refreshing tartness.
- •• **Crooked Tree Pale Ale**–American-style pale ale, brewed with Cascade hops.
- •••• **Dark Horse Special Reserve Black Bier**–Full bodied, malty sweet and roasty with a chocolaty finish. 7.5% ABV.

BREWERY NOTES
Family restaurant atmosphere. Try the hummus appetizer–it's delicious.

Mt. Pleasant, Michigan
MOUNTAIN TOWN STATION

506 West Broadway, Mt. Pleasant, MI 48858; phone 517-775-2337
Web Address: www.mountaintown.com
Type: Brewpub
Near: Between Oak Street and the railroad tracks
Opens: 11:30 a.m. daily
Prices: Expensive
Opening Date: 1996
Most Popular Beer: Gamblers Golden Ale and Cow Catcher Red
Brewing System: 15 barrel

BEER LIST
- **Gamblers Golden Ale**
- **Cow Catcher Red Ale**
- ••• **Iron Horse I.P.A.**–Unfiltered. Assertively hopped with Northern Brewers.
- **Hobo's Breath Brown Ale**
- •• **Loose Caboose Porter**–Lightly malty and roasty. Slightly sour with a hint of chocolate in the finish.
  Chip River Weizen
  River Bend Bock
  Railyard Raspberry Wheat
  Steam Engine Stout (Oatmeal Stout)
  Oil Baron's Barley Wine

BREWERY NOTES
Railroad station theme. Beers are served quite cold.

Northville, Michigan
BONFIRE BISTRO & BREWERY

39550 7 Mile Road, Northville, MI 48167; phone 248-735-4570
E-mail: bonfire19@aol.com
Type: Brewpub
Near: Haggerty Road
Opens: 11 a.m. daily
Prices: Average to expensive
Opening Date: March 1999
Most Popular Beer: Vulcan's Vienna ale
Brewing System: 10 barrel, Global

BEER LIST
Firelight Lager
Burning Brand Bitter
Vulcan's Vienna Ale
Promethean Porter
Smoldering Coals Imperial Stout–Cask conditioned.

BREWERY NOTES
A rotating 5th tap, plus two cask conditioned beers are always available.

Novi, Michigan
LOCAL COLOR BREWING COMPANY

42705 Grand River, Novi, MI 48375; phone 248-349-2600
E-mail: kenb@localcolor.com
Web Address: www.localcolor.com
Type: Microbrewery and Restaurant
Near: Novi Road
Opens: 11:30 a.m. daily
Prices: Average
Opening Date: January 1998
Most Popular Beer: Smooth Talker Pilsner
Brewing System: 30 barrel, fully automated 4 vessel Beraplan

BEER LIST

- ••• **Social Climber Light Lager**–Crystal clear with a fresh aroma and hop character. It's tough to make a distinctive light beer, but this one qualifies.
- ••• **Smooth Talker Pilsner**–Good interpretation of the style, soft malt body, not heavily hopped.
- ••• **Old Friend Stout**–Nice medium-bodied stout, served at proper temperature. Dark copper, with amber hues. Malty, and roasty, with hints of chocolate. Not particularly complex, but flavorful.
- •• **No.VI Brown Ale**–Suggestions of chocolate.
- •• **Tomboy Red** (Red Lager)–Mildly malty, with a lightly buttery texture.
- ••• **Corporate Jim's Pale Ale**–Caramel-like malt character, lightly hopped.
- •••• **I.P.A.**–A hop-head's delight, lots of grapefruit-like bitterness and flavor.

BREWERY NOTES

A very high-tech German lager house. Malt and hops are imported from Germany. The atmosphere is difficult to describe; it simply must be seen. It is visually interesting, if not cozy, and no expense has been spared. The eclectic décor goes with a general theme of urban diversity; that diversity is mirrored by a menu featuring buffalo burgers, steak, prime rib, wood-fired pizza, seafood, and more. A fun, unique place to enjoy a beer. Live entertainment. Cigar room and beer garden.

Okemos, Michigan
TRAVELERS CLUB INTERNATIONAL RESTAURANT AND TUBA MUSEUM

2138 Hamilton Road, Okemos, MI 48864; phone 517-349-1701
E-mail: traveler@travelerstuba.com
Web Address: www.travelerstuba.com
Type: Brewpub
Near: Corner of Okemos and Hamilton roads
Nearby City: Lansing
Opens: 8 a.m. daily
Prices: Average
Opening Date: Brewing since summer 1999
Brewing System: 1 barrel and 10 barrel

BEER LIST
···· **Lavender Lager**–This is a very unique and full flavored beer, brewed with lavender grown out on their own patio. An unfiltered beer, with an interesting bitterness, and a spicy finish reminiscent of all-spice. Too intensely flavored to be characterized as refreshing, it exhibits a strong perfumy lavender and spicy nose. What is refreshing, however, is to see a brewery that's adventurous enough to offer such an unusual beer.
Adagio Ale
Sousaphone Stout

BREWERY NOTES
Initially they are brewing with a small 1-barrel system, with plans to move up to a 10-barrel brewhouse. Two house brewed beers and 5 Michigan brewed beers on tap, plus over 50 imported and domestic bottled beers to choose from.

Excellent food from an eclectic "traveling" menu, featuring authentic world cuisine. Located ten minutes from Michigan State University. The building started out as a hardware store when it was built in 1950 and was converted to a Miller's Ice Cream Parlor around 1959. The restaurant was founded in 1982 by a group of local artist-entrepreneurs.

Oscoda, Michigan
WILTSE'S BREW PUB AND FAMILY RESTAURANT

5606 North F-41, Oscoda, MI 48750; phone 517-739-2231
Type: Brewpub
Near: 1 mile from US-23 on F-41
Opens: 7 a.m. daily
Prices: Average
Opening Date: Started brewing December 1994
Brewing System: 4 barrel, Pico

BEER LIST
 Paul Bunyan Ale
 Old Au Sable Weizenbier
 Blue Ox Stout

BREWERY NOTES
Paul Bunyan theme. Pub/family restaurant atmosphere.

Paradise, Michigan
TAHQUAMENON FALLS BREWERY AND PUB

Camp 33, M-123, Paradise, MI 49768, phone 906-492-3300
Web Address: www.exploringthenorth.com
Type: Brewpub
Near: Tahquamenon Falls State Park
Opens: 10 a.m. daily
Prices: Average
Opening Date: December 1996
Most Popular Beer: Lumberjack Lager
Brewing System: 10 barrel, Bohemian

BEER LIST
- •• **Lumberjack Lager** (Blonde Lager)–Nicely balanced and clean lager. Lightly malty with a delicate hop finish.
- • **Blueberry Ale**–Usually offered at the time of the annual blueberry festival, in late August.
  White Pine Pilsner
  Falls Tannin (Red Ale)
- • **Black Bear Stout** (Irish Dry Stout)

BREWERY NOTES
In Michigan's Upper Peninsula. This is the only brewery located *in* a state park that I am aware of. Most of their business comes from tourists, not regulars. With this in mind, and to keep things interesting, they rotate their beers constantly, never offering a regular lineup of beers.

Gorgeous brewery with lightly stained cedar ceiling and a large, beautiful central stone fireplace. Definitely worth a visit, if only for the atmosphere. While none of the beers are especially challenging, they are all well made, with no off-flavors, and the food is excellent. Oh . . . and while you're there, you might want to check out Tahquamenon Falls, only a short walk from the brewery.

Pontiac, Michigan

For Pontiac breweries, also see Auburn Hills.

Pontiac, Michigan
BO'S BREWERY AND BISTRO

51 North Saginaw, Pontiac, MI 48342; phone 248-338-6200
Type: Brewpub
Near: Corner of East Huron and North Saginaw
Opens: 11 a.m. Monday-Saturday; noon Sunday
Prices: Average
Opening Date: August 1996
Most Popular Beer: Bo's Blonde
Brewing System: 15 barrel

BEER LIST
- **Bo's Blonde**
- **Whitelake Wheat** (American Wheat)–Brewed with 30% wheat malt.
- •• **North 51 Pale Ale**–Cirtusy American-style pale ale.
- •• **Seminole Hills Red**–Medium bodied red with a slightly spicy, dry finish.
- •• **Dr. Conger's Porter**–Silky, malty, and roasty, with a definite chocolate character.
  Bald Mountain Nut Brown

BREWERY NOTES
A variety of single malt Scotch, as well as martinis and cigars, are available.
Good vegetarian selection. Big screen TV.

Pontiac, Michigan
KING BREWING COMPANY

985 Oakland Avenue, Pontiac, MI 48340; phone 248-745-5900
Web Address: pw1.netcom.com/~kboyse/index.htm
Type: Microbrewery and Taproom
Near: East of Telegraph Road
Open: Tap room hours are 4-9 p.m. Thursday-Friday; 2-7 p.m. Saturday
Opening Date: August 1995
Brewing System: 15 barrel

BEER LIST
    Royal Amber
••• **Crown Brown Ale**–Light-bodied and lightly nutty with hints of chocolate.
•• **Pale Ale** (American-style Pale Ale)–Citrusy hop character.
    Pontiac Porter
••• **Two Fisted Old Ale** (Barley Wine)–Deep red caramel color, with a malty sweet and vinous nose. The heavy maltiness is lightly balanced by the hops, leaving a beer that's sweet without being syrupy. The most striking flavor is a wine-like fruitiness that is quite complex. 9% ABV.
    Cherry Ale–Brewed with Michigan tart cherries.
    Honey B
• **Red Ale**

Port Huron, Michigan
QUAY STREET BREWING COMPANY

330 Quay Street, Port Huron, MI 48060, phone 810-982-4100
E-mail: contact@quaybrew.com
Web Address: www.quaybrew.com
Type: Brewpub
Near: Huron Street
Opens: 11:30 a.m. daily; closed Sunday between October 4 and May 5.
Prices: Average
Opening Date: July 1997
Most Popular Beer: Cream Ale
Brewing System: 7 barrel, DME

BEER LIST
- •• **Michigan Cream Ale**
- • **Blue Water Pale Ale**
- ••• **Quay Street Wheat** (Bavarian-style Wheat)–Unfiltered, German hops. Cloudy, with a light banana and clove nose and flavor. Refreshingly sour
- ••• **Raspberry Wheat**–Unfiltered.
- ••• **Tug B-Oatmeal Stout**–Smooth, rich and chocolaty, with coffee-like finish. My favorite of the bunch
- •• **Euro-Lager**–Assertively hopped lager.
  Nutting Better Nutbrown Ale
  Ed's Red
  Porter

BREWERY NOTES
Family restaurant/pub atmosphere. Live blues every Saturday. Growlers, and half barrels to go. Located in a former cosmetology college.

Rochester, Michigan
ROCHESTER MILLS BEER COMPANY

400 Water Street, Rochester, MI 48308
Phone: 248-650-5080
E-mail: seavra@aol.com
Web Address: www.royaloakbrewery.com
Type: Brewpub
Near: Downtown Rochester, between East Third and East Fourth
Nearby City: See Detroit
Opens: 11 a.m. daily
Prices: Average
Opening Date: June 1998
Most Popular Beer: Rochester Red and Lazy Daze Lager
Brewing System: 15 barrel, Specific Mechanical

BEER LIST

••• **Lazy Daze Lager**–Straw golden and clear. Soft malt body with a somewhat dry finish. Easy drinking.

•• **Water Street Wheat** (Bavarian-style Wheat)–Unfiltered. Lightly sour with mild clove and banana characteristics. Medium bodied, very refreshing.

•• **Big Horn Sheep Bitter**–Designed as a light British session beer. Not a great deal of British character, but still enjoyable.

•• **Rochester Red**–Caramel sweetness. Quite enjoyable.

•••• **Cornerstone I.P.A.**–Obviously potent, medium-bodied pale ale. A significant maltiness is well balanced by hops. Finishes decidedly bitter.

•••• **Michigan Mild**–Medium brown with an extraordinarily nutty finish, reminiscent of walnuts. Hints of chocolate and caramel. Excellent!

••• **Sacri-licious Stout** (Dry Stout)–Slightly sweet malty body, with hints of coffee and chocolate.

••• **Porter**–Strong caramel malt character, very much in the tradition of a London Porter.

•••• **Oktoberfest**–Caramel malt sweetness with a strong spiciness. Excellent.

•• **Black Lager**–Rich, near black in color. Silky with some chocolate and molasses flavors.

BREWERY NOTES

An excellent brewpub. Above average beers that, although not intense, are all good examples of the styles they represent. Up to 10 beers on tap at a time.

Rochester Mills Beer Company (cont.)

Located in the historic western knitting mills of Rochester. The building was originally a knitting mill from the 1800s, where sheep were sheared and the wool was made into usable products. The building was renovated in 1998 and the brewpub retains the original floor, columns, beams, and ceiling. Cavernous restaurant, with full view of the brewery and the serving tanks. Over a dozen TVs scattered throughout the area for easy viewing on game day, yet it avoids a sports bar atmosphere.

Beer appreciation nights feature a different style of beer the third Monday of each month.

Scotch, whiskey, bourbon, brandy, cognac, wine, and Belgian beers also available. Billiards, and a cigar/martini lounge. Live music 5 nights a week.

Same ownership as the Royal Oak Brewery.

Royal Oak, Michigan
ROYAL OAK BREWERY

215 East Fourth Street, Royal Oak, MI 48067; phone 248-544-1141
Web Address: www.royaloakbrewery.com
Type: Brewpub
Near: South Main Street
Nearby City: See Detroit
Opens: 11:30 a.m. Monday-Saturday; noon Sunday
Prices: Average
Opening Date: 1995
Most Popular Beer: Northern Light
Brewing System: 14 barrel

BEER LIST
- ••• **The Northern Light** (Kölsch)–Good interpretation of the style. Soft malt body and light ale fruitiness.
  Fourth Street Wheat (Bavarian-style Wheat)
- •• **Pleszure's I.P.A.**–Strong hop flavor with a moderate bitterness.
- ••• **Brewhouse E.S.B.**–Good English character, with a proper bitter finish. Well done.
- •• **Drunk'in Druid Red**–Much stronger than a typical brewpub red, 6.75% ABV.
  Pappy's Porch-Sippin' Porter

BREWERY NOTES
Free non-alcoholic beverages for designated drivers. Excellent Belgian bottled beer list. Wood-fired pizza with beer-grain dough as an option. Excellent varied menu. Multiple TVs and one big screen.

Saginaw, Michigan
FRANKENTROST BREWPUB

8640 East Holland Road, Saginaw, MI 48601; phone 517-771-0055
E-mail: brownjsf@concentric.net
Type: Brewpub
Near: 5 miles east of I-75, 6 miles north of Frankenmuth
Opens: Noon daily
Opening Date: March 1998. Scheduled to start brewing by late 1999.
Brewing System: Half barrel, custom system.

BREWERY NOTES
Excellent bottled beer list featuring many Michigan brewed beers. Housed in a building dating back to 1872 that has been a bar, hotel, blacksmith shop, dance hall, post office, and general store. Sells homebrewing and winemaking supplies.

Sanford, Michigan
SANFORD LAKE BAR AND GRILL

3770 Bailey Road, Sanford, MI 48657; phone 517-687-5620
E-mail: Slbg87@aol.com
Web Address: members.aol.com/slbg87/index.html
Type: Brewpub
Near: West River Road
Opens: 4 p.m. Tuesday-Thursday; 11:30 a.m. Friday-Saturday;
noon Sunday; closed Monday
Most Popular Beer: Sharlyn's Red Crown
Brewing System: 15 gallon

BEER LIST
  Sharlyn's Red Crown
  Mel's Irish Ale
  Dick's Gold Crown Lager
  Brown Dog American Ale
  Corbat's Porter

BREWERY NOTES
One of the smallest brewpubs in the region. They brew their beers from extract and always have three house brewed beers on tap. A variety of domestic and imported beers are also available. Voted "Best Perch Dinner" in *Midland Daily News.*

Southfield, Michigan
COPPER CANYON BREWERY

27522 Northwestern Highway, Southfield, MI 48034
Phone: 248-223-1700
Type: Brewpub
Near: 11 Mile and Northwestern Service Drive
Nearby City: See Detroit
Opens: 11:30 a.m. daily; noon Sunday
Prices: Expensive
Opening Date: 1998
Most Popular Beer: Northwestern Gold
Brewing System: 15 barrel

BEER LIST

•• **Northwestern Gold**–Soft malt body and fresh hop balance. Good light ale.
•• **Copper Canyon Alt**–A reddish copper. Clean with a slight bitter finish.
••• **Devils Peak Pale Ale**–Domestic hops provide a huge grapefruit-like flavor in this beer. Despite the big hop character, it's not a particularly bitter I.P.A.
••• **Buffalo Jump Stout** (Coffee Stout)–Rich and silky with distinct coffee and chocolate characteristics.
•• **Kilkenny Irish Ale**–Light bodied and refreshing with a nice bitter finish.
•• **London Porter**–Silky and roasty.

BREWERY NOTES

Try the sweet and spicy "Root 696" rootbeer. Two pool tables, multiple TVs and one big screen for entertainment.

Spring Lake, Michigan
OLD BOYS BREWHOUSE

971 West Savidge Street, Spring Lake, MI 49456; phone 616-850-9950
E-mail: info@old-boys.com
Web Address: www.old-boys.com
Type: Brewpub
Near: Junction of US-31 and M-104
Opens: 11 a.m. daily; closed Sunday
Prices: Expensive
Opening Date: October 1997
Brewing System: 10 barrel, DME

BEER LIST

- •• **Rockethound Pale Ale**–Cascade dry hopped. Crisp and clean with a light grapefruit flavor and moderate bitterness.
- •• **Waterdog Wheat** (American Wheat)–Unfiltered. Needs more dog.
- •• **Grayhound Ale**–Lightly hopped. Good training wheels beer.
- •• **Rover's Waggin' Red**–Light caramel sweetness, nicely balanced.
- •• **Old Boys' Brown Ale**–A bit big bodied for the style, closer to a porter. Light chocolaty characteristics. Very nice.
- ••• **Doghouse Porter**–My favorite of the bunch. Medium to full bodied. Malty and silky, slightly sour, and lightly roasty, with a highly enjoyable bittersweet chocolate finish.
  Raspberry Wheat
  Raspberry Gold
  Golden Sour–Their golden ale blended with lime.

BREWERY NOTES
Nicely executed dog theme. Good food and beer. Several menu items are prepared with their house beer. Growlers, 5 and 15.5 gallon kegs to go. They plan to bottle their beer in the future. Handcrafted sodas.

St. Joseph, Michigan
LIGHTHOUSE DEPOT
RESTAURANT AND BREWPUB

1 Lighthouse Lane, St. Joseph, MI 49085; phone 616-98-BREWS
Type: Brewpub
Near: Marina
Prices: Average
Opens: 11 a.m. Monday-Saturday; closed Sunday
Opening Date: September 1997
Most Popular Beer: St. Joe's Light
Brewing System: 15 barrel, DME

BEER LIST
- •• **St. Joe's Light**
- • **Red Sky Night**
- • **Raspberry Ale**
- • **3 Knights Porter**
- • **Pale Ale**
- • **I.P.A.**
- •• **Mild Ale**
- •• **Stout**

BREWERY NOTES
Outstanding food from an eclectic menu. Considering the quality and portion size, the prices are very reasonable.

The beers lack a great deal of character and distinctiveness. They are all fine, no off flavors, but most are brewed to the extreme light end of the spectrum.

The Lighthouse Depot dates back to 1893. It served as the primary supply and buoy repair depot for all of Lake Michigan. The lighthouse was vacated in 1993 and added to the U.S. Department of Interior National Register of Historical Places in 1994. A beautiful restoration. Brick walls and original ash hardwood floor, with a centrally positioned brewery. Try to get a table on the upper level.

Traverse City, Michigan
For Traverse City breweries, also see Williamsburg.

Traverse City, Michigan
MACKINAW BREWING COMPANY

161 East Front Street, Traverse City, MI 49684; phone 616-933-1100
Type: Brewpub
Near: Corner of Cass and Front Street
Opens: 11 a.m. daily
Prices: Average to expensive
Opening Date: June 1997
Most Popular Beer: GT Golden
Brewing System: 7 barrel, Peter Austin

BEER LIST
- **GT Golden**
- **Peninsula Pale Ale** (American-style pale ale)–Lightly buttery and mildly sweet with a moderate hop counterbalance.
- **Red 8 Ale**–Malty with a light spicy finish.
- **Beadle's Best Bitter**
- •• **Pig Stout** (Irish Stout)–Traditionally served via nitrogen tap.

BREWERY NOTES
Located in the historic Beadle building, built in 1892. It spent time as a Big Boy restaurant before housing the brewery. In addition to their five house beers they offer a rotating sixth tap.

Traverse City, Michigan
NORTH PEAK BREWING COMPANY

400 West Front Street, Traverse City, MI 49684; phone 616-941-PEAK
Type: Brewpub
Near: Corner of Hall and Front streets
Opens: 11 a.m. daily
Prices: Average to expensive
Opening Date: 1997
Most Popular Beer: Pale Ale
Brewing System: 10 barrel

BEER LIST
- •• **North Lights Golden Ale**–Grainy and mildly sweet. Hop balance from European Saaz and Hallertauer.
- •• **North Peak Pale Ale** (American-style Pale Ale)–American Magnum hops perform the bittering work, and leave a nice finish.
- • **Steelhead Red Ale**
- •• **Mission Point Porter**–Caramel malt quality, with a hint of chocolate in the finish. Fuggles aroma hops.
- •• **Shirley's Irish Stout**
- •••• **Get Fuggled I.P.A.**–Easily their best beer. Cask conditioned and served via beer engine. Excellent English cask ale character. Smooth, mellow and lightly sour. True to the modern day English I.P.A. style, it is actually not very bitter. It successfully made my heart ache for London.

BREWERY NOTES
Housed in an old, quite large turn-of-the-century candy factory. Cask conditioned ales served via English beer engine. In addition to their five house beers, they offer a rotating sixth tap. Good bottled beer list, featuring over 20 beers from Michigan and around the world.

Wood-fired pizza oven.

Warren, Michigan
DRAGONMEAD MICROBREWERY

14600 East Eleven Mile Road, Warren, MI 48089
Phone: 810-776-9428
Type: Microbrewery and Taproom
Near: Groesbeck Highway
Open: Taproom hours are 4-9 p.m. Thursday-Friday; noon-9 p.m. Saturday
Opening Date: May 1998
Brewing System: 3 barrel

BEER LIST
- •• **Lancelot's Jousting Ale**–Centennial and Saaz hops. Nicely balanced American pale. Subtle hop finish. The Saaz hops are an interesting choice for an American-style pale ale; they add a bit of spiciness to the beer.
- • **Crooked Door Pale Ale** (American-style Pale Ale)–Cascade hops. A bit buttery with a subtly stronger hop finish than the Lancelot's Jousting Ale.
  Mariann's Honey Brown–Hallertauer, Fuggles and Mt. Hood hops.
- •• **Breath of the Dragon English Bitter**–Galena and Williamette hops. A well-balanced bitter. A bit big bodied for the style.
  Sir William's Extra Special Bitter–Galena and Fuggles hops.
  English Mild Ale–Fuggles hops.
- •• **Positively Woody's Porter**
- ••• **Earl Spit Stout**–E. Kent Golding hops and roasted barley and chocolate malts. Fermented with Irish Ale yeast. A wonderfully rich, malty nose. Silky mouthfeel, slightly sour, and chocolaty. 6.2% ABV.
- ••• **Dragonmead Altbier**–Clear and medium copper colored. It starts mildly malty and has a slight metallic hop character that builds nicely on the sides of the tongue.
- ••• **Nagelweiss Wheat Beer** (Bavarian-style wheat)–Strong banana nose. Spicy finish.
- •• **Bill's Witbier**–Mt. Hood hops, spiced with orange peel and coriander.
- ••• **Dubbel Dragon Ale**–Sweet and malty nose with a clear banana character. The nose predicts the flavor well. Also present is a clearly Belgian fruity complexity. 7.2% ABV.

Dragonmead Brewery (cont.)

Dead Monk Abbey Ale–Belgian candi sugar, Pilsen, Aromatic and Caramunich malts. E. Kent Goldings, Mt. Hood and Saaz hops. 8.0% ABV.

•••• **Final Absolution Belgian-style Tripel**–Malty, with a touch of banana and cinnamon. Light amber colored. A very nice interpretation of a Tripel. 10% ABV.

•••• **90 Shilling Scotch Export Ale**–Imported Scottish ale malt, peat-smoked barley, Goldings and Fuggles hops. More smoked malt character than in the 60, also bigger bodied and maltier. 7.8% ABV.

••• **60 Shilling Scotch Ale**–Overly big bodied and malty for the style. Skillfully light addition of peat-smoked malt, just enough to blend nicely with the malty body and create an interesting overall character. 5.7% ABV.

•• **Imperial Stout**–Six-row barley, roasted chocolate and caramel malts, East Kent Goldings hops. Malty and slightly fruity nose, with a flavor that follows suit. Lacking in the complexity of some of the classic examples of the style, but very tasty nonetheless. 7.5% ABV.

BREWERY NOTES

Small batch sizes enable this outstanding little microbrewery to offer a phenomenal number of beers on tap. At the time of my visit, they were offering over 20–one tough beer sampler to get through! One of their long-term goals is to brew, and offer on tap, every style of beer that is recognized by the Great American Beer Festival. The truly impressive aspect of this brewery is not simply the number of beers offered; rather it is their commitment to brewing "true-to-style" beers. They employ over 50 different varieties of grains, and multiple varieties of hops and yeast, to brew their beers with the traditional ingredients that each style calls for.

Webberville, Michigan
MICHIGAN BREWING COMPANY

2582 M-52 North, Webberville, MI 48892
Phone: 517-521-3600
Type: Microbrewery and Taproom
Near: I-96 and M-52
Opens: Noon daily
Opening Date: January 1996
Most Popular Beer: I.P.A.
Brewing System: 30 barrel

BEER LIST
Michigan Amber Lager
• **Dunkel**
••• **Hefe-Weizen**–Banana, clove, and hints of vanilla
•••• **Pale Ale**
•••• **I.P.A.**–A celebration of hops. Big and resinous, it is loaded with hop aroma and flavor. For any beer novice curious about what hops smell and taste like, this beer will provide an education. 7% ABV.
•••• **Brown Ale**–Easily quaffable. The light maltiness and easy drinkability goes great with all those free peanuts. Very good example of the style.
•••• **Peninsula Porter**–Roasty, and chocolaty, with a nicely assertive hop bitterness in the finish. Excellent.
•••• **Oatmeal Stout**–Rich and creamy, slightly sour with chocolate and molasses notes.
Seasonals:
Oktoberfest
Christmas Bock
Scotch Ale
•••• **Pilsner**–Crystal clear and light golden in color with a fresh hoppy nose. Well attenuated with a wonderful bitter/salty finish.
•• **Belgian Tripel**–Banana fruitiness and a spicy dry finish.

BREWERY NOTES
With their utilitarian atmosphere, this is a wonderful place to sit back and enjoy a great locally brewed beer. Small non-smoking bar area, separate smoking area, and a large barrel of free peanuts. At the time of my visit they had nine beers on tap. Also available are two soft drinks: Miners Brew Root Beer, and Big Wheel Orange Cream Soda. Lots of beer-to-go options: growlers, party pigs, ½ barrels, 1/6 barrels, and kegs. Tours available.

Westland, Michigan
FIRE ACADEMY BREWERY AND GRILL

6677 North Wayne Road, Westland, MI 48185; phone 734-595-1988
E-mail: gariley@msn.com
Type: Brewpub
Near: Ford Road
Nearby City: See Detroit
Opens: 11 a.m. Monday-Saturday; noon Sunday
Prices: Average
Opening Date: December 1997
Most Popular Beer: Golden Axe Ale
Brewing System: 10 barrel

BEER LIST
- **Golden Axe Ale** (Blonde Ale)
- **Smoke-Eater Wheat**
  Wildfire Berry
- **Chef's Amber Ale**
- **Maltese Cross Beer** (Brown Ale)
  Pike Pole Porter
  Hook and Ladder Scotch Ale
- **Sergeant Stout**

BREWERY NOTES
Firefighting theme.

Williamsburg, Michigan
TRAVERSE BREWING COMPANY

11550 US-31, Williamsburg, MI 49690; phone 616-264-9343
Type: Microbrewery
Near: Townline Road, just south of Elk Rapids
Opens: 10 a.m. Monday-Friday
Opening Date: January 1996
Most Popular Beer: Manitou Brand Amber Ale
Brewing System: 14 barrel, Peter Austin

BEER LIST
   Sleeping Bear Brown Ale
••• **Old Mission Lighthouse Ale**–Distinct ale fruitiness, with a nice hop aroma and a mild lingering bitter finish. An excellent crisp and refreshing pale ale.
•• **Manitou Brand Amber Ale**–Medium bodied with a spicy dry finish.
•••• **Stout**–Full-bodied, virtually black with subtle dark ruby hues, and a foamy tan head. Chocolaty sweetness combined with a roasty bitterness and coffee-like qualities.
   Shandy–An ale with lemon concentrate added.

BREWERY NOTES
Traverse Brewing Company beers all exhibit a praiseworthy dense and rocky head, forming lasting peaks and valleys. They also brew many contract beers for various businesses. Bottled beer available to go.

102

Wyandotte, Michigan
SPORTS, A 50s BAR AND GRILL

166 Maple Street, Wyandotte, MI 48192; phone 734-285-5060
Type: Brewpub
Near: Maple and Second Street in downtown Wyandotte
Nearby City: See Detroit
Opens: 11 a.m. Monday-Saturday; noon Sunday
Prices: Average
Opening Date: Brewing since December 1998
Brewing System: 3 barrel

BEER LIST

- ••• **Golden Ale**–Grainy and moderately hopped with a lingering finish. A bit more challenging than a typical golden.
- •• **Wheat** (American Wheat)
- •• **Raspberry Wheat**
- •• **Amber Ale**–Copper colored. Spicy finish.
- •• **Stout**

BREWERY NOTES

As the name implies, it is a sports bar with a 50s motif. A fun atmosphere, with 50s music and a center bar right out of a 50s ice cream parlor. The addition of a brewpub seems a strange fit. Good list of beers on tap, including Guinness Stout, and various Michigan brewed beers.

Burgers, ribs, and pizza. Won award for best burgers from *News Heritage* newspapers readers poll. Root beer in frosted mugs. Live Blues every Friday and Saturday. Nineteen TVs, 2 big screens.

BREWERIES OF OHIO

OHIO "BEST OF GREAT LAKES" BREWERIES:
Barley's Brewing Company (page 119)
Diamondback Brewery (page 114)
Great Lakes Brewing Company (page 115)

ADDITIONAL RECOMMENDED OHIO BREWERIES:
Brewhouse Pub and Grille (page 125)
Crooked River Brewing (page 113)
Hoster Brewing (page 122)
Main Street Brewery (page 110)
Main Street Brewing (page 111)
Maumee Bay Brewing (page 129)
Teller's of Hyde Park Micropub and Eatery (page 112)
Watson Brothers Brewhouse (page 108)

Akron, Ohio
For Akron breweries, also see Copley.

Akron, Ohio
LIBERTY STREET BREWING

1238 Weathervane Lane, Akron, OH 44313, phone 330-869-2337
Type: Brewpub
Near: Merriman Road
Opens: 11:30 a.m. Monday-Saturday; closed Sunday
Prices: Average to Expensive
Opening Date: December 1994
Most Popular Beer: Dragonslayer
Brewing System: 15 barrel

BEER LIST
- • **Paul Bunyan**
- •• **Valley Fog** (California Common style)
- • **El Nino Mild Ale**
- •• **Dragonslayer** (Scottish Export style)
- •• **Black Silk** (Robust Porter)
  Sir Winston (English Pale Ale)

BREWERY NOTES
Upscale restaurant featuring American cuisine with Creole and Mediterranean influences. Large selection of wines to choose from, in addition to port, sherry, cognac, and single malt Scotch.

Athens, Ohio
O'HOOLEY'S PUB AND BREWERY

24 West Union Street, Athens, OH 45701; phone 740-594-2739
Type: Brewpub
Near: Court Street
Opens: 1 p.m. Monday-Saturday; closed Sunday
Prices: Inexpensive
Opening Date: Started brewing November 1996
Most Popular Beer: Ohio Pale Ale
Brewing System: 7 barrel

BEER LIST
Golden Ale
Raspberry Wheat
E.S.B.
Ohio Pale Ale
Bong Water (hemp ale)
Winter Ale (old ale)–5.5% ABV
Scottish Ale

BREWERY NOTES
As of early 1999 they did not yet offer a full menu. Primarily pub fare, sandwiches, fries, hot dogs, etc.

Bedford Heights, Ohio
BUCKEYE BREWING COMPANY

25200 Miles Road, Bedford Heights, OH 44146; phone 216-292-2739
Type: Microbrewery and Taproom/Brew-on-Premises
Near: Richman Road
Nearby City: See Cleveland
Opens: 11 a.m. Tuesday-Friday; noon-5 p.m. Saturday-Sunday
Opening Date: June 1997
Most Popular Beer: Hippy I.P.A. and Old Mamouth Stout
Brewing System: 3 barrel

BEER LIST
Downtown Brown (American Brown)
Buckeye Blue (American Lager)
Buckeye Red (Amber Ale)
Wheat Cloud (Hefe-Weizen)
Old Mamouth Stout
Hippy IPA
Oktoberfest

Blue Ash, Ohio
WATSON BROTHERS BREWHOUSE (QUEEN CITY BREWING)

4785 Lake Forest Drive, Blue Ash, OH 45242; phone 513-563-9797
E-mail: info@qcbrewing.com
Web Address: www.qcbrewing.com
Type: Brewpub
Near: Corner of Pfeiffer Road and Lake Forest Drive
Nearby City: See Cincinnati
Opens: 11 a.m. Monday-Saturday; 1 p.m. Sunday
Prices: Average
Opening Date: June 1996

BEER LIST
- •• **Hallertau Honey Rye**–Citrusy and spicy seasonal. Creamy mouthfeel, spicy rye character.
- •• **Woody's American Wheat**–Unfiltered, very smooth, with a refreshing sourness.
- •• **Abigail's Amber**–Well-balanced beer.
- ••• **Aviator Red**–Excellent light bodied beer, nice Tettnanger finish, very smooth.
- ••• **Main Street Pale Ale**–Wonderful cascade aroma, bitterness, and finish.
- •• **Toby's New Zealand Dark** (Brown Ale)–Chocolaty and hoppy finish.
- •••• **Main Street Steamboat Stout**–Malty and roasty aroma that perfectly predicts the flavor. Hints of chocolate.

BREWERY NOTES
Great food and beer. Beer served at the proper temperature. Attractive center bar area. Shares beer recipes with other Queen City Brewing sites: Main Street Brewery, Main Street Brewing Company, and Teller's of Hyde Park Micropub and Eatery

Centerville, Ohio
THIRSTY DOG BREWING COMPANY

45 West Alex-Bell Road, Centerville, OH 45459; phone 937-438-8081
Type: Brewpub
Near: Loop Road
Opens: 11 a.m. Monday-Friday; noon Saturday-Sunday
Opening Date: June 1998
Most Popular Beer: Air Light (Blonde Ale)
Brewing System: 10 barrel, J.V. Northwest

BREWERY NOTES
Located in a suburb of Dayton. See North Canton Thirsty Dog Brewing Company.

Cincinnati, Ohio

For Cincinnati breweries, see also Blue Ash.

Cincinnati, Ohio
BARREL HOUSE BREWING

22 East Twelfth Street, Cincinnati, OH 45210; phone 513-421-2337
Type: Brewpub
E-mail: brewers@barrelhouse.com
Web Address: www.barrelhouse.com
Near: Walnut and 12th, in the downtown area
Opens: 11 a.m. Tuesday-Friday; noon Saturday and Sunday;
 closed Monday
Prices: Inexpensive
Opening Date: June 1995
Most Popular Beer: Cumberland Pale Ale and Hocking Hills Hefe-Weizen
Brewing System: 15 barrel, Century

BEER LIST
Year Round:
- **Redlegg Ale** (Special Bitter)
- **Honeysuckle Blond**
- **Cumberland Pale Ale** (I.P.A.)–Lightly hopped for an I.P.A.
- **Hocking Hills Hefe-Weizen**
- **SternWheeler Stout**
   Flying Pig Pilsner
Seasonals:
   Duveneck's Dortmunder
   Barrelhouse Bock
   Powderhorn Porter
   Cherry Porter
   Oktoberfest Lager
   Belgian Christmas Ale
   DunkelWeizen
   Broadway Commons Cream Ale

BREWERY NOTES
Cask conditioned ales on Friday and Saturday. Unusual in that there is always at least one lager on tap, usually two or three. German styles are prominent due to Cincinnati's German brewing heritage. Growlers, quarter barrels and half barrels to go.

Located in a renovated historic factory in Cincinnati's Main Street Entertainment District. A long, copper braided bar wraps around the open brewery. Creative casual cuisine, featuring gourmet pizzas, fresh salads, and specialty sandwiches. Live music on weekends, and areas for pool and darts. Cask conditioned ales on Friday and Saturday.

Cincinnati, Ohio
HOLY GRAIL BREWERY AND GRILL

13 West Charlton Street, Cincinnati, OH 45219; phone 513-861-7821
E-mail: holygrail@fuse.net
Web Address: www.beercamp.com
Type: Microbrewery and Restaurant
Near: U of C, between Jefferson and Short Vine streets
Opens: 11 a.m. daily
Prices: Average
Opening Date: November 1996
Most Popular Beer: Pious Pale Ale
Brewing System: 7 barrel

BEER LIST
- **Wild Blue Yonder** (American Wheat)–Served with whole blueberries, intense blueberry flavor.
- **Pious Pale Ale**
- **Black Cat** (Dark Lager)
- **Porter**
- **Red**
- **Raspberry Wheat**
- **OPV** (Bavarian Lager)
  Pig's Eye Porter
  Blonde
  Holy Grail Nut Brown

Cincinnati, Ohio
MAIN STREET BREWERY
(QUEEN CITY BREWING)

1203 Main Street, Cincinnati, OH 45210; phone 513-665-4677
E-mail: info@qcbrewing.com
Web Address: www.qcbrewing.com
Type: Brewpub
Near: East 12th Street
Opens: 11 a.m. Monday-Friday; noon Saturday; closed Sunday
Opening Date: December 1994

BEER LIST & BREWERY NOTES
For a list of some of their beers, see Watson Brothers Brewhouse in Blue Ash, Ohio. Shares beer recipes with other Queen City Brewing sites: Main Street Brewing, Watson Brothers Brewhouse, and Teller's of Hyde Park Micropub and Eatery.

Cincinnati's first brewpub. Voted "best brewpub" by readers in the October 1998 issue of *Cincinnati Magazine*.

Cincinnati, Ohio
MAIN STREET BREWING
(QUEEN CITY BREWING)

218 West McMicken, Cincinnati, OH 45214; phone 513-421-2739
E-mail: info@qcbrewing.com
Web Address: www.qcbrewing.com
Type: Microbrewery

BEER LIST & BREWERY NOTES
For a list of some of their beers, see Watson Brothers Brewhouse in Blue Ash, Ohio. Shares beer recipes with other Queen City Brewing sites: Main Street Brewery, Watson Brothers Brewhouse, and Teller's of Hyde Park Micropub and Eatery

Cincinnati, Ohio
ROCK BOTTOM BREWERY #10

10 Fountain Square, Cincinnati, OH 45202; phone 513-621-1588
Type: Brewpub
Near: Between 5th and 6th streets
Opens: 11 a.m. Monday-Saturday; noon Sunday
Prices: Average to expensive
Opening Date: August 1996
Most Popular Beer: Cincinnati American Light
Brewing System: 12 barrel, J.V. Northwest

BEER LIST
  Cincinnati American Light
  Crosley Field Pale Ale
  White Tiger Wheat
  Raccoon Red
  Brown Bear Brown
  River Boat Stout

BREWERY NOTES
Large Colorado based brewpub chain with many locations. Twelve or more specialty beers every year that vary seasonally. Generally 7-8 beers on tap at any one time.

Cincinnati, Ohio
TELLER'S OF HYDE PARK MICROPUB & EATERY (QUEEN CITY BREWING)

2710 Erie Avenue, Cincinnati, OH 45208; phone 513-321-4721
E-mail: info@qcbrewing.com
Web Address: www.qcbrewing.com
Type: Brewpub
Near: Edwards
Opens: 11 a.m. Monday-Saturday; 10 a.m. Sunday
Prices: Expensive
Opening Date: October 1995
Most Popular Beer: Woody's American Wheat
Brewing System: 4 barrel

BEER LIST & BREWERY NOTES
For a list of some of their beers, see Watson Brothers Brewhouse in Blue Ash. Most of the beer they serve is brewed at Main Street Brewing. They share beer recipes with other Queen City Brewing sites: Main Street Brewery, Main Street Brewing, and Watson Brothers Brewhouse.

The building used to be the Hyde Park Savings bank and is cleverly decorated throughout with miscellaneous bank paraphernalia. Located in an attractive area of downtown Cincinnati nestled in with many interesting shops.

Cleveland, Ohio
For Cleveland breweries, also see these nearby cities: Bedford Heights, Westlake.

Cleveland, Ohio
CLEVELAND CHOPHOUSE AND BREWERY

824 West St. Clair Avenue, Cleveland, OH 44113; phone 216-623-0909
Type: Brewpub
Near: West 6th
Opens: 11:30 a.m. daily
Opening Date: May 1998
Most Popular Beer: Pale Ale
Brewing System: 8 barrel, J.V. Northwest

BEER LIST
 Bohemian Pilsner–Saaz hops
 American Pale Ale
 Nut Brown
 Irish Stout–Served on nitrogen.

BREWERY NOTES
Usually two rotating taps in addition to their regular lineup. Located in the warehouse district.

Cleveland, Ohio
CROOKED RIVER BREWING

1101 Center Street, Cleveland, OH 44113; phone 216-771-BEER
E-mail: SKdanckers@AOL.com
Web Address: www.crookedriver.com
Type: Microbrewery and Taproom
Near: Between Fall Street and Merwin, across from the Flat Iron Cafe in
the Flats
Open: Tap room hours 11 a.m.-2:30 a.m.
Opening Date: August 1994
Most Popular Beer: Black Forest Lager
Brewing System: 30 barrel, Century

BEER LIST
•• **Gold**–Smooth and light.
•• **Black Forest Lager** (Munich Helles)–Smooth, hot-day thirst quencher.
••• **Settler's Ale** (American Amber)- Light malt body with a moderate hop
zing.
••• **Cool Mule Porter**–Yakima hops.
Seasonals:
• **Irish Red**
Doppelbock–Cold lagered for 2 1/2 months.
Yuletide Ale (Christmas Ale)–Cascade and Eroica Hops. Spiced ale.
Ballpark Draft–Served only at Jacobs Field.
Arena Draft–A beer brewed for Cleveland basketball at the arena.

BREWERY NOTES
Free self-serve peanuts; toss the shells on the floor. Happy hour 3-7 daily,
pints $2. Tours available.

Cleveland, Ohio
DIAMONDBACK BREWERY

724 Prospect Avenue, Cleveland, OH 44115
Phone: 216-771-1988
E-mail: bmorgan@stratos.net
Web Address: www.diamondbackbrewery.com
Type: Brewpub
Near: East 9th Street
Opens: 11:30 a.m. Monday-Friday; 4:30 p.m Saturday; 11 a.m. Sunday
Prices: Average
Opening Date: 1996
Most Popular Beer: Black Diamond Pale Ale
Brewing System: 15 barrel

BEER LIST
- •• **White Diamond Pilsner**–100% Saaz hops.
- ••• **Black Diamond Pale Ale**–Chinook and Cascade hops. Nicely made American-style pale ale.
- ••• **Snowshovel I.P.A.**–Chinook, Centennial, and Cascade hops. Bigger bodied than the pale ale, moderately bitter with nice hop complexity and flavor.
- ••• **Rattler Red** (Vienna Lager)–Smooth and lightly caramelly.
- •• **Steelcut Oatmeal Stout**
- ••• **Fuzzknuckle Peach Ale**–378 pounds of peaches and 84 pounds of apricots in each batch. Nice fruit beer with a wonderful apricot finish, not too sweet.
- • **Old Leghorn** (Old Ale)–Disappointing. Malty sweet without much complexity. Possibly hampered by Ohio's ludicrous 6% ABW limit on beer.
  Framboise Lambic
- •••• **Lambic**–Wonderfully tart cranberry lambic. Complex, with a great zing in the finish.
  Union Porter

BREWERY NOTES
Diamondback offers cask conditioned ales and brews truly outstanding lambic beers, plus they make the best pub fries I have sampled. The lambics alone are worth going out of your way for. Old hardwood floors enhance the comfortable and warm atmosphere, with pool tables on the spacious second floor. Voted best restaurant in Cleveland by *Cleveland Magazine*.

CLEVELAND, OHIO

Cleveland, Ohio
GREAT LAKES BREWING COMPANY

2516 Market Avenue, Cleveland, OH 44113
Phone: 216-771-4404
Web Address: www.greatlakesbrewing.com

Type: Regional Brewery and Restaurant
Near: West 25th Street and Lorain Avenue
Opens: 11:30 a.m. Monday-Saturday; 3 p.m. Sunday
Prices: Average to expensive
Opening Date: September 1988
Most Popular Beer: Dortmunder Gold
Brewing System: 7 barrel Century and 75 barrel Mueller

BEER LIST

•••• **Dortmunder Gold**–Cascade and Hallertau hops. Foamy white head and flowery hop nose with a touch of sweetness. Soft and smooth, with spicy hop notes and a mild caramel malt balance. Very easy drinking and yet quite flavorful.

•••• **Eliot Ness** (Vienna-style)–Hallertau hops.

•••• **Edmund Fitzgerald Porter**–Brewed with Northern Brewer, Kent Golding, and Cascade hops. Rocky and coarse head. Medium-bodied, complex and roasty, with coffee and chocolate notes. Unusually assertive hop finish for a porter.

•••• **Moon Dog Ale** (Best Bitter)–A fine example of the style, and a great session beer. Hopped with Northern Brewer and Kent Golding.

•••• **Burning River Pale Ale**–Named for the infamous 1969 Cuyahoga incident. Assertive spicy, resinous hop nose and flavor thanks to generous use of Cascade hops. Slightly buttery mouthfeel and a roasted malt character, with a very light ale fruitiness and an enduring bitter finish.

••• **Conway's Irish Ale**–Available mid-January to late March. Kent Golding hops.

••• **Christmas Ale**–Assertively spiced and warming seasonal, 6% ABV.
The Holy Moses (Belgian Wit)–Brewed with Hallertau hops, orange peel, coriander, and camomile flower. A summer seasonal named after Moses Cleaveland, who founded Cleveland in 1796.

•• **Munich Dunkel**

•• **Pale Bock**
Oktoberfest–Hallertau and Liberty hops.
The Commodore Perry India Pale Ale

(continued)

115

Great Lakes Brewing Company (cont.)
BREWERY NOTES

In 1988 this century-old Victorian building, in the historic Ohio City District, became Ohio's first brewpub since Prohibition. Since then, Great Lakes Brewing has become one of the most frequently honored, awarded, and nationally known breweries in the Midwest. Recently they have expanded into their new 75-barrel brewhouse. The expansion has increased their yearly capacity to 30,000 barrels, with an ultimate potential to brew upwards of 100,000 barrels. Happily, their beer is now available outside of Ohio.

The restaurant features a nicely varied menu, complete with helpful recommendations for the beer that best compliments their various entrees.

"Beer School" meets Wednesday nights from 5-7 p.m., where students can learn about beer and tour the $6.5 million brewery. Irish session music is offered on the first Sunday of each month.

Cleveland, Ohio
JOHN HARVARD'S BREW HOUSE

1087 Old River Road, Cleveland, OH 44113; phone 216-623-2739
Web Address: www.johnharvards.com
Type: Brewpub
Near: On the east bank of the Flats, between Main and Front
Opens: 11:30 a.m. daily
Prices: Average
Opening Date: September 1997
Most Popular Beer: John Harvard's Pale Ale
Brewing System: 15 barrel

BEER LIST
- •• **John Harvard's Pale Ale**–Light bodied with a nice grapefruit hop finish.
- •• **Newtown Nut Brown**–Easy drinking dark ale.
- •• **Pilgrim's Porter**–Tasty, mildly sweet porter. Chocolaty finish.
- • **Brewhouse Alt**
- • **Mid-Winters Old Ale**–Fairly weak old ale. Possibly fettered by Ohio's ridiculous 6% ABW limit on beer.
- •• **U.S. Grant's Presidential Ale** (I.P.A.)–A bigger bodied and maltier version of their pale ale.

BREWERY NOTES
An eastern U.S. brewpub chain with a constantly rotating beer selection that includes one or two beers from each family of styles. The Nut Brown and Pale Ale are always available. Every Wednesday is "Firkin Wednesday"; customers volunteer to tap the fresh firkin of cask-conditioned beer. Cozy brick interior decorated with stained glass and attractive solid oak tables.

Cleveland, Ohio
ROCK BOTTOM BREWERY #8

2000 Sycamore Street #260, Cleveland, OH 44113; phone 216-623-1555
Web Address: www.rockbottom.com
Type: Brewpub
Near: Located in a building called the Powerhouse
Opens: 11:30 a.m. daily
Prices: Average to expensive
Opening Date: September 1995
Most Popular Beer: Wheat Ale
Brewing System: 12 barrel, J.V. Northwest

BEER LIST
  Wheat Ale (American Wheat)
  Cleveland American Light
  Powerhouse Pale
  Riverbend Red Ale
  Buzzard Brown
  Terminal Stout

BREWERY NOTES
In "The Flats" area of Cleveland. Always two specialties on tap in addition
to the regulars. Twelve or more specialty beers every year that vary seasonally. Generally 7-8 beers on tap at anyone time. Large Colorado based brewpub
chain with many locations.

Cleveland, Ohio
WESTERN RESERVE BREWING

4130 Commerce Avenue, Cleveland, OH 44103; phone 216-361-2888
E-mail: wrbrew@msn.com
Web Address: www.wrbrew.com
Type: Microbrewery
Near: 2 blocks north of East 40th and Chester
Open: 10 a.m.-6 p.m. Monday-Friday
Opening Date: July 1997
Most Popular Beer: American Wheat
Brewing System: 20 barrel, J.V. Northwest

BEER LIST
Year round:
   Western Reserve American Wheat
   Western Reserve Amber Ale
   Western Reserve Nut Brown
Seasonals:
   Western Reserve Lake Effect Winter Ale (Scotch ale)
   Western Reserve Bockzilla (Bock Beer)
   Western Reserve Cloud Nine (Belgian Wit Beer)

BREWERY NOTES
They brew in adherence with the Reinheitsgebot. Brewery tours by appointment. Local brewery that sells only within the state of Ohio. Recipient of numerous national and international awards in first year of production.

Columbus, Ohio
BARLEY'S BREWING COMPANY

467 North High Street, Columbus, OH 43215
Phone: 614-228-2537
Type: Brewpub
Near: Goodale
Opens: 11 a.m. Monday-Saturday, noon Sunday
Prices: Average
Opening Date: November 1992
Most Popular Beer: Pale Ale
Brewing System: 10 barrel, Century

BEER LIST
••• **Pale Ale**–Spicy pale with a citrusy hop quality.
• **Pilsner**
••• **MacLenny's Scottish Ale**–Nice balance with a mild finish. A great session beer.
•••• **Christmas Ale** (Golden Ale with black honey, ginger, orange zest, and spices)–Big ginger spike in this complex seasonal.
•••• **Auld Curiosity Ale** (Old Ale)–A big beer. Strong malt character, with an obvious alcohol kick. Brewed with the addition of English molasses. My favorite of the bunch. Inspired, in part, by Theakston's Old Peculiar. Excellent interpretation.
•• **Queen Ann Stout**–Dry stout with a rather light roasted malt character.
Irish Rogue (Red Ale)
J. Scott Francis E.S.B.–Named after the brewer.
Wheat (Bavarian-style Wheat)
Angelo's Crooked Sky Rye
Bee's Wing Honey Wheat
Ivan Porter
Ol' Ron's Surly Oatmeal Stout
Alexander's Russian Imperial Stout
Centennial India Pale Ale

BREWERY NOTES
Excellent beers served at proper temperature. American pub cuisine. Live bands in their basement called Barley's Underground. See also Barley's Smokehouse in Grandview.

119

Columbus, Ohio
BARLEY'S SMOKEHOUSE

1130 Dublin Road, Columbus, OH 43212; phone 614-485-0227
Type: Brewpub
Near: Grandview Avenue
Opens: 11 a.m. Monday-Saturday; noon Sunday
Opening Date: 1998
Most Popular Beer: Scottish Ale
Brewing System: 10 barrel, Century

BEER LIST
  Scottish Ale
  Cherry Porter
  Smoked Stout
  Tavern Ale (English Pale Ale)–Modeled after Bass Ale
  Pilsner
  Pale Ale
  E.S.B.

BREWERY NOTES
BBQ and Cajun cuisine. They share recipes with Barley's Brewing Company in Columbus.

Columbus, Ohio
COLUMBUS BREWING

535 Short Street, Columbus, OH 43215; phone 614-224-3626
Web Address: www.cmrestaurants.com
Type: Microbrewery and Restaurant
Near: Near Liberty in the heart of the historic Brewery District
Opens: 11:30 a.m. Monday-Saturday
Prices: Expensive
Opening Date: July 1988
Most Popular Beer: Columbus Pale Ale
Brewing System: 30 barrel

BEER LIST
- •• **Columbus Golden Ale**–Grainy, mild hop bite. Nice starter beer.
- ••• **Columbus Pale Ale**–Thin-bodied with a strong citrusy, slightly resinous hop character.
- • **Columbus Nut Brown**–Light-bodied with a prickly mouthfeel, thin chocolaty flavor.
- •• **Columbus 1859 Porter**–Silky, slightly sour porter with a nice chocolate finish.
- •• **Santa's Little Helper**–Unfiltered pale ale.
- •• **Columbus Apricot Ale**–Very strong apricot nose, and a pleasing (not overwhelming) apricot flavor, supported by a medium bodied ale.

BREWERY NOTES
Columbus's first brewpub. They brew only ales and always have five house beers available, along with rotating specialty beers. All their beers are filtered, except for the specialties, which are for in-house consumption only. Their beer can be found in many local establishments on draft.

Columbus, Ohio
HOSTER BREWING

550 South High Street, Columbus, OH 43215; phone 614-228-6066
Web Address: www.hosters.com
Type: Brewpub
Near: Corner of Hoster Street in the Brewery District of German Village
Opens: 11 a.m. Monday-Saturday; 11:30 a.m. Sunday
Prices: Average
Opening Date: November 1989
Most Popular Beer: Gold Top
Brewing System: 20 barrel, Beraplan

BEER LIST
- **Gold Top** (Dortmunder Export style)
- **Amber Lager** (Vienna-style)
- ••• **Rev. Purley Pale Ale**–Big grapefruit nose and hop flavor, a bite of grapefruit in every sip.
- •• **Eagle Dark** (Bock)–Six malts and four hop varieties.
- **Kölsch Beer**
- •••• **Doppelbock**–An excellent and warming doppelbock. Strong alcohol and full bodied malt flavor.
  Belgian White
  Scottish Ale
  Maibock

BREWERY NOTES
Brick walls, hardwood floors, and exposed ceiling create a warm and comfortable atmosphere. Live music every Friday and Saturday night. Great food and a selection of wines and single malt Scotch.

Spent grain is donated to Ohio State University cattle research as feed.

Copley, Ohio
THIRSTY DOG BREWING COMPANY

37 Montrose West, Copley, OH 44333; phone 330-670-9272
Type: Brewpub
Near: Route 18
Nearby City: See Akron
Opening Date: November 1998
Most Popular Beer: Air Light
Brewing System: 10 barrel, J.V. Northwest

BEER LIST
Air Light (Blonde Ale)

BREWERY NOTES
See North Canton Thirsty Dog Brewing Company

Delphos, Ohio
MEYER BREWING

900 Elida Avenue, Delphos, OH 45833; phone 419-695-5560
Type: Microbrewery
Web Address: meyerbrewing.com
Opening Date: March 1997
Most Popular Beer: Meyer Copper Ale
Brewing System: 4 barrel, customized dairy tanks

BEER LIST
  Meyer Copper Ale
  Wheat (Bavarian-style Wheat)

BREWERY NOTES
Small-scale brewery, family owned and operated. No retail sales. Brewery tours upon request. Bottled beer is available throughout Ohio.

Garrettsville, Ohio
GARRETT'S MILL BREWING

8148 Main Street, Garrettsville, OH 44231; phone 330-527-5849
Type: Brewpub
Near: One block east of the corner of Highways 82 and 88
Opens: Hours vary seasonally
Prices: Expensive
Opening Date: June 1995
Brewing System: 3 barrel

BEER LIST
•• **Uncle Eric's Pale Ale** (American-British hybrid)
  Honey Porter
•• **Hazelnut Brown Ale**–A very light colored brown ale with a nice flavorful hazelnut character.
  Golden Ale
  Stout

BREWERY NOTES
Alessi's Reistorante shares the same area as the brewery. Garrett's Mill was constructed in 1804 next to the Silver Creek waterfalls. Using what is reportedly the largest operating water wheel in the world, it continues to grind flour. Alessi's Reistorante and the Garrett's Mill Brewing Company were added to the building in 1995.

Kent, Ohio
BLIMP CITY BREWERY

330 Tallmadge Road, Building F, Kent, OH 44240; phone 330-673-2537
E-mail: bierwiz@aol.com
Web Address: www.blimpcity.com
Type: Microbrewery
Near: Just west of I-76
Open: Call for hours
Opening Date: December 1998
Most Popular Beer: Akron/Macon Ale
Brewing System: 10 barrel, Century

BEER LIST
> **All American Blonde**–American style pale ale spiced with Centennial hops.
> **K-Ship Kölsch**
> **Akron/Macon Ale** (Alt-style)

BREWERY NOTES
The brewery exhibits a love of airships. Blimp City's website explains the reasons behind their dirigible theme. Retail sales are limited to kegs, 15½ - gallon, and 2½-gallon sizes. The brewery is family owned and operated.

Marblehead, Ohio
FRONTWATERS RESTAURANT AND BREWING

8620 East Bayshore Road, Marblehead, OH 43440; phone 419-798-8058
Web Address: www.frontwaters.com
Type: Microbrewery and Restaurant
Near: Bayshore and Englebeck streets
Opens: Call for hours. Closed in the winter.
Opening Date: May 1996
Most Popular Beer: Marblehead Lighthouse
Brewing System: 10 barrel, New World

BEER LIST
> **Marblehead Red**
> **Port Clinton Porter**
> **Lightkeeper's Ale** (Bavarian-style Wheat)–Unfiltered. Weihenstephan yeast strain.
> **Gale Warning Ale** (I.P.A.)
> **Crystal Rock Doppel Bock**
> **Belgian Abbey Ale**
> **Russian Imperial Stout**
> **Coriander Amber Lambic**–Wheat, coriander, apricots, and pears.

Niles, Ohio
OHIO BREWING

5790 Youngstown Warren Road, Niles, OH 44446; phone 330-505-0061
Type: Brewpub
Near: Route 46, also called Canfield/Niles Road
Opens: 11:30 a.m. daily
Prices: Expensive
Opening Date: July 1997
Most Popular Beer: Verich Gold
Brewing System: 10 barrel

BEER LIST
- **Verich Gold** (Kölsch)
- **Cardinal Ale**
- **Alt-ernative Amber Ale** (German Alt)
- **Buckeye Brown Ale**
- •• **Steel Valley Stout**
  Ohio Fest

BREWERY NOTES
Sampler served on Ohio shaped platter.

North Canton, Ohio
BREWHOUSE PUB AND GRILLE

4262 Portage Street NW, North Canton, OH 44720; phone 330-966-7447
Type: Brewpub
Near: Near I-77
Opens: 11 a.m. Monday-Friday; 11:30 a.m. Saturday; closed Sunday
Prices: Inexpensive
Opening Date: November 1996
Most Popular Beer: Galloping Ghost Amber Ale and Crazy Legs India
   Pale Ale
Brewing System: 5 barrel

BEER LIST
- **Golden Boy Pale Ale**–A light pale ale.
- •• **Galloping Ghost Amber Ale**–Willamette and Cascade hops.
- ••• **Crazy Legs India Pale Ale**–Bittered with Northern Brewer and Centennial, and dry hopped with more Centennial. Nice coarse Centennial aroma, flavor and bitterness.
- ••• **Night Train Porter**–Nice dark malt character. Chocolaty and malty sweet.
- •• **Papa Bear Stout**–A rather sweet stout, served on nitrogen tap.
  Mad Stork Winter Ale

BREWERY NOTES
Canton's first brewpub. In addition to the house brews, they have 20 additional beers on tap, including other Ohio microbrews.

North Canton, Ohio
THIRSTY DOG BREWING COMPANY

5419 Dressler Road NW, North Canton, OH 44720; phone 330-497-2739
Type: Brewpub
Near: Everhard, behind Bob Evans
Opens: 11 a.m. Monday-Saturday; noon Sunday
Prices: Average
Opening Date: February 1997
Most Popular Beer: Airship Ale
Brewing System: 10 barrel, J.V. Northwest

BEER LIST
Golding's Retriever (Pale Ale)–East Kent Goldings and American Cascade hops.
- **Mixed Breed** (Black & Tan)–A blend of the Golding's Retriever and Old Leghumper.
- **Airship Ale** (Blonde Ale)
- **Dierdorfer** Gold (Bohemian Pilsner)
- **Robinson's English Ale**
- **Labrador Lager** (Oktoberfest)
- **Stud Service Stout** (Oatmeal Stout)
Irish Setter Red
Airship Light (light beer)–100 calories.
Raspberry Ale
Anniversary Ale
Old Leghumper (Porter)
Raspberry Leghumper (Porter with Raspberry)

BREWERY NOTES
Dog theme restaurant, in case the name didn't give it away. Beer samplers are served on a large dog-bone platter. A chain brewpub with 3 locations (see Copley and Centerville). Each location shares 8 standard beers and several location-specific beers. They offer over 14 beers on tap at any one time.

Portsmouth, Ohio
MAULT'S BREWPUB

224 Second Street, Portsmouth, OH 45662; phone 740-354-6106
Type: Brewpub
Near: Highway 52
Opens: 11 a.m. Friday-Saturday; 3 p.m. Monday, Wednesday, and
Thursday; 1 p.m. Sunday; closed Tuesday
Prices: Average
Opening Date: February 1997
Most Popular Beer: Portsmouth Pilsner
Brewing System: 10 barrel

BEER LIST
Portsmouth Pilsner
Redbird Ale
Babes Brown Porter
Spartan Export (Dortmunder Export-style)

Rocky River, Ohio
ROCKY RIVER BREWING COMPANY

21290 Center Ridge Road, Rocky River, OH 44116; phone 440-895-2739
Type: Brewpub
Near: Wagar, near the Westgate Mall
Opens: 11:30 a.m. daily
Prices: Expensive
Opening Date: July 1998
Most Popular Beer: Copper's Gold
Brewing System: 7 barrel, Century

BEER LIST
Brad Street Bitter (E.S.B.)
Chocolate Thunder (Schwarzbier)
Copper's Gold (Kölsch)
Hilter Kilter (Scotch Export)
Dragon's Milk (Oatmeal Stout)
Jimmy's Purple Haze (Blackberry Wheat)
Nickel Plate Porter
Pale Ale
Pilgrim Pumpkin
Santa's Little Helper (Christmas Ale)
The Sub Chaser (Hefe-Weizen)
IPA
The Westlake (Raspberry Wheat)
Old Detroit Alt
Dry Dock Amber Alt–High gravity German style alt.

127

Srongsville, Ohio
THE MAD CRAB

12492 Prospect Road, Strongsville, OH 44136; phone 216-238-4677
Type: Brewpub
Near: Route 82 after Pearl
Open: Closed Mondays
Prices: Expensive
Opening Date: November 1996
Most Popular Beer: Wheat and Pilsner
Brewing System: 7 barrel, Continental

BEER LIST
- **Blue Whale Wheat**
- **Pirate's Pilsner**
- **Sturgeon Stout**

BREWERY NOTES
Seafood brewpub with a nautical theme.

Strongsville, Ohio
RINGNECK BREWING COMPANY

15143 Pearl Road, Strongsville, OH 44136; phone 216-846-4677
Type: Microbrewery and Brew-On-Premise
Near: State Route 42 (Pearl Road) and Route 82, in Town Square plaza.
Open: 2-9 p.m. Monday-Friday; 9 a.m.-6 p.m. Saturday
Opening Date: December 1995
Most Popular Beer: Porter
Brewing System: 3 barrel, Price Schonstrom

BREWERY NOTES
Bottled beer to go, sold from the microbrewery only. Kegged beer is available at local restaurants and bars.

They share the same location as "The Brew Kettle," a brew-on-premises. The Brew Kettle offers the chance to brew your own beer using professional equipment. Many recipes to choose from.

Toledo, Ohio
MAUMEE BAY BREWING

27 Broadway, Toledo, OH 43602; phone 419-241-1ALE
Type: Brewpub
Near: Oliver and Summit streets
Opens: 11 a.m. Monday-Friday; noon Saturday and Sunday
Prices: Average
Opening Date: November 1995
Most Popular Beer: Buckeye Boys Blond
Brewing System: 15 barrel

BEER LIST
- ••• **Buckeye Boys Blonde**–Great thirst quencher, a flavorful blonde.
- •• **Broadway Pale**–Well balanced, very mild bitter finish.
- •• **Blitzen Holiday Ale**–A seasonal brown ale spiced with orange zest, cinnamon, and honey. A enjoyable combination of a pleasing body, warming alcohol, mild flavor, and complimentary spices.
- •• **Fallen Timbers Red**–A very light-bodied red enhanced by a spicy hop flavor. Quite satisfying.
- •• **Boyer Brown**
- •••• **Frogtown Dunkel**–An excellent Dunkel, my favorite beer of the bunch. Nice body and subtle smokiness, with a lingering chocolate finish.
  Belgian Ale
  High Level Vienna Lager
  I.P.A.
  Lost Peninsula Pilsner
  Major Oliver's Oatmeal Stout
  Oliver House Porter
  Wee Bock
  Willy's Overland Wheat
  ESB
  Oktoberfest

BREWERY NOTES
Originally the Oliver House, a hotel built in 1859. Five million dollars later it's a beautifully renovated brewpub with brick walls, hardwood floors, three levels, and a great cozy decor.

The four "house beers" are always available, the blonde, pale ale, red, and brown. They also offer two rotating taps from a rich selection of seasonals and specialty beers.

Uniontown, Ohio
BURKHARDT BREWING COMPANY

3700 Massillon Road, Uniontown, OH 44685; phone 330-896-9200
Type: Brewpub
Near: 1/4 mile past a McDonald's. Look for "Shops of Green." It's in the center atrium.
Opens: 11 a.m. Monday-Saturday; 4 p.m. Sunday
Prices: Average to expensive
Opening Date: April 1990
Most Popular Beer: North Star
Brewing System: 7 barrel

BEER LIST
- **North Star**
- **White Cliff** (British-style Pale Ale)
- **Eclipse** (Scottish-style Ale)
- **Mug Ale** (Nut Brown ale)
- **Irish Red**
- **Raspberry Ale**–Sweet and quite raspberry intense. Much like a wine cooler, virtually no beer character, but often that's how brewpub fruit beers are intended to be.
- • **Cask Conditioned Bitter**–Their best beer.
  Peach Ale
  Wheat Beer
  Porter
  Oktoberfest
  Bock
  Stout
  Trappist Style Ale

BREWERY NOTES
Impressive menu. Several costly entrees such as prime rib, New York strip steak, and grilled salmon. They usually have between 4 and 6 beers on tap at any one time. Large wine list.

Excellent staff, very helpful and attentive. The Burkhardt family has been brewing beer in Akron since 1876. The current brewery is owned by the fourth generation of that family.

Westlake, Ohio
WALLABY'S BREWING

24400 Sperry Drive, Westlake, OH 44145; phone 216-808-3552
E-mail: AussieBrew@aol.com
Web Address: www.wallabys.com
Type: Microbrewery
Nearby City: See Cleveland
Open: 9 a.m.-5 p.m. Monday-Friday
Opening Date: August 1997
Brewing System: 50 barrel

BREWERY NOTES
Bottled beer distribution. See Wallaby's Grille and Brewpub.

Westlake, Ohio
WALLABY'S GRILLE AND BREWPUB

30005 Clemmens Road, Westlake, OH 44145; phone 216-808-1700
E-mail: AussieBrew@aol.com
Web Address: www.wallabys.com
Type: Brewpub
Nearby City: See Cleveland
Near: Just north of I-90 exit 156 (Crocker-Basset exit)
Opens: 11 a.m. daily
Prices: Average
Opening Date: May 1995
Most Popular Beer: Great White Wheat
Brewing System: 10 barrel, Bohemian

BEER LIST
- •• **Great White Wheat** (American Wheat)
- •• **Ayers Rock**–American-style pale ale. A light interpretation of the style. Subtle, yet refreshing, citrusy hop finish.
- • **Big Red Roo** (Strong Ale)–British and Belgian malts, and Aussie hops. A tasty beer, but too light for a strong ale. Possibly hindered by Ohio's absurd 6% ABW limit. Nice caramel malt character with a spicy hop finish.
- •• **Matilda Pale**
- • **Cherry Porter**–Not much porter character, probably better described as simply a cherry ale. Smooth cherry flavor.
- •• **Billabong Brown**
- •• **Oatmeal Stout**
  Raspberry Ice
  Croco-Pale Ale
  Cranberra Cream Ale
  Maori Milk Stout

BREWERY NOTES
Australian theme restaurant, complete with Aussie artifacts. Sampler served on large boomerang platter. Dart boards.

Willoughby, Ohio
WILLOUGHBY BREWING COMPANY

4057 Erie Street, Willoughby, OH 44094, phone 440-975-0202
Type: Brewpub
Near: Glenn Avenue
Opens: 11 a.m. Monday-Saturday, 4 p.m. Sunday
Prices: Average to expensive
Opening Date: February 1998
Most Popular Beer: Willoughby Wheat (American Wheat)
Brewing System: 15 barrel, J.V. Northwest

BEER LIST
   Railway Razz (Raspberry Wheat)
   Willoughby Wheat
   Lost Nation Pale Ale (British-style)
   Northern Trail Nut Brown Ale (British-style)
   Last Stop Stout (Dry Stout) – Served on nitrogen tap.

Xenia, Ohio
MIAMI TRAIL BREWING COMPANY

1455 South Patton Street, Xenia, Ohio 45385; phone 937-374-3660
Web Address: www.miamitrail.com
Type: Microbrewery and Taproom
Near: Located in Xenia Industrial Park, on State Route 68 south
Opens: 10 a.m. Monday-Saturday; closed Sunday
Opening Date: March 1998
Most Popular Beer: Miami Trail Golden Ale
Brewing System: 30 barrel, Century

BEER LIST
   Miami Trail Golden Ale
   Miami Trail Pale Ale
   Miami Trail Red Ale (Brown Ale)
   Miami Trail Stout Ale

BREWERY NOTES
Miami Valley's only brewery. Beer is also distributed in Kentucky. Antique oak and brass bar. Complete line of brewery paraphernalia in the "Miami Trail Shop."

BREWERIES OF WISCONSIN

WISCONSIN "BEST OF GREAT LAKES" BREWERIES

Capital Brewing Company (page 158)
Great Dane Pub and Brewing Company (page 155)
New Glarus Brewing Company (page 166)
Sprecher Brewing Company (page 147)

ADDITIONAL RECOMMENDED WISCONSIN BREWERIES

Appleton Brewing Company (page 136)
Brewery Creek Brewing (page 162)
Gray's Brewing Company (page 150)
Green Bay Brewing Company (page 144)
Harbor City Brewing Company (page 168)
Joseph Huber Brewing Company (page 164)
Lakefront Brewery (page 159)
Minocqua Brewing (page 163)
Stevens Point Brewery (page 171)

Appleton, Wisconsin
APPLETON BREWING COMPANY/
ADLER BRAU

1004 South Old Oneida Street, Appleton, WI 54915; phone 920-731-3322
Type: Microbrewery and Restaurant
Near: Just south of the Fox River
Opens: 11 a.m. daily
Prices: Average
Opening Date: 1989
Most Popular Beer: Tailgate Amber
Brewing System: 7 barrel

BEER LIST
- • **Eagle Lager**
- • **Cherry Creek**
- • **Marquette Pilsner**
- • **Tailgate Amber**
- • **Downtown Brown**
- •• **Divers Ale** (Brown Ale)
- •• **Weiss**–Very light flavored Bavarian-style.
- • **Oktoberfest**–Light for the style.
- •• **Classic Porter**–Light porter.
- •• **Fox Classic River Ale**–Moderately hopped.
- ••• **Oatmeal Stout**–Smooth with roasty, coffee overtones.
- ••• **Pumpkin Spice**–Pumpkin pie filling by the pint, strong cinnamon spice.

BREWERY NOTES
Occupies a building that housed the original Appleton Brewing company, dating back to 1859. The brewery closed during prohibition. Today the brewery is on the main floor and the restaurant is in the basement. The entire building is nicely decorated with beer paraphernalia of all types.

Twelve beers on tap. Bottled beer and growlers to go. Voted "favorite microbrewery" by the readers of *Wisconsin Trails* magazine.

Appleton, Wisconsin
FOX RIVER BREWING COMPANY AND RESTAURANT

Fox River Mall, 4301 West Wisconsin Avenue, Appleton, WI 54915
Phone: 920-991-0000
E-mail: info@foxriverbrewing.com
Web Address: www.foxriverbrewing.com
Type: Brewpub
Near: In the Fox River Mall, just west of Highway 41
Opens: 11 a.m. daily
Prices: Average
Opening Date: November 1997
Most Popular Beer: Winnebago Wheat and Caber Tossing Scottish Ale
Brewing System: 13.5 barrel

BEER LIST
- Fox River Golden Ale
- Winnebago Wheat (Bavarian-style Wheat)–60% wheat malt.
- Paine's Lumberyard Pilsner
- Buzzin' Honey Ale–35% wheat malt and pure Wisconsin honey.
- Foxtoberfest (Oktoberfest)
- Duck Blind Rye–Lightly spicy.
- Fox Tail Amber Ale–Dry hopped.
- Caber Tossing Scottish Ale
  Titan Porter
- Trolleycar Stout

BREWERY NOTES
Six-packs, growlers, and kegs to go.

Ashland, Wisconsin
SOUTH SHORE BREWERY AND RAILYARD PUB

400 Third Avenue West, Ashland, WI 54806; phone 715-682-9199
Type: Brewpub
Near: Junction of US-2 and State Highway 13
Opens: 11 a.m. daily
Opening Date: May 1995
Most Popular Beer: South Shore Nut Brown Ale
Brewing System: 3 barrel, DME

BEER LIST
  South Shore Nut Brown Ale
  South Shore Pale Ale
  South Shore Honey Beer
  South Shore Porter
  South Shore Bavarian Wheat
  South Shore Oktoberfest
  South Shore Applefest Ale (Fruit Beer/Mead)–Locally grown apples,
     brewed with 21% honey.
  South Shore Rhodes Scholar Stout
  South Shore Silver Street Gold

BREWERY NOTES
Two separate restaurants are housed in the same building. One offers value
priced casual dining and the other offers upscale fine dining.

Black River Falls, Wisconsin
PIONEER BREWING COMPANY

320 Pierce Street, Black River Falls, WI 54615; phone 715-284-7553
Web Address: www.pioneerbrewing.qpg.com
Type: Microbrewery
Opens: Call ahead for tours
Opening Date: June 1997
Most Popular Beer: Pioneer Lager and Wood Duck Wheat
Brewing System: 20 barrel, J.V. Northwest

BEER LIST
Pioneer Lager (Bavarian-style)
Pioneer Pale Ale
Pioneer Black River Red
Wisconsin Brewing Wood Duck Wheat
Wisconsin Brewing White Tail Cream Ale
Wisconsin Brewing Rainbow Red
Wisconsin Brewing Badger Porter

BREWERY NOTES
In 1998 Pioneer Brewing Company purchased the brands and beer recipes from the Wisconsin Brewing Company, which had been devastated by floods two years in a row. They plan to keep the two brands separate. The building they occupy was originally a brewery that operated from 1856 to prohibition.

Bonduel, Wisconsin
SLAB CITY BREWING COMPANY

W3590 Pit Lane, Bonduel, WI 54107; phone 715-758-BEER
Type: Microbrewery
Near: Highline Road
Opens: Variable hours
Opening Date: May 1996
Most Popular Beer: Esker Alt
Brewing System: 4 barrel, customized dairy tanks

BEER LIST
Esker Alt
Old 47 Pale Ale (American-style Pale Ale)
Xena Bock
Milk House Stout (Dry Stout)–So named because the brewery is located in an old milk house.

BREWERY NOTES
Growlers available at local grocery stores. About a dozen tap accounts were spread out around Wisconsin as of late 1998.

Chilton, Wisconsin
ROWLAND'S CALUMET BREWERY

25 North Madison, Chilton, WI 53014; phone 920-849-2534
Type: Brewpub
Near: On Highway 57, just north of Highway 151
Opens: 2 p.m. Tuesday-Thursday; noon Friday-Sunday; closed Mondays
Opening Date: September 1990
Most Popular Beer: Dark and Seasonals
Brewing System: 3 barrel, J.V. Northwest

BEER LIST
- **Calumet Pilsner**
- **Calumet Wheat**
- **Calumet Amber**
- **Calumet Dark**

Seasonals:
   Calumet Bock
   Calumet Rye
- **Calumet Oktoberfest**
   Total Eclipse

BREWERY NOTES
Reportedly the third-smallest brewery in the nation. Rustic, simple atmosphere. Pool table.

The original Calumet Brewing Company closed in 1942 for failure to pay beer excise taxes, ending nearly 90 years of operation. The building that currently houses the Calumet Brewing Company has a different history. It used to house Chilton's fire station. During the dark years of prohibition it served as a dress shop, and later became a tavern.

Chippewa Falls, Wisconsin
JACOB LEINENKUGEL BREWING COMPANY

1 Jefferson Avenue, Chippewa Falls, WI 54729; phone 715-723-5557
Web Address: leinie.com
Type: Regional Brewery
Opens: Call for hours
Opening Date: 1867
Most Popular Beer: Leinenkugel's Red Lager
Brewing System: 160 barrel copper brew kettle

BEER LIST
Year Round:
   Leinenkugel's Original Lager (American Light Lager)
 •• **Leinenkugel's Red Lager**
 •• **Leinenkugel's Honey Weiss Bier**–Somewhat sour with a lightly sweet finish, just a hint of honey.
  • **Leinenkugel's Northwoods Lager** (Oktoberfest)–Perfumy, light bodied.
   Leinenkugel's Auburn Ale
   Leinenkugel's Creamy Draft
   Leinenkugel's Hefe-weizen–60% malted wheat and German Perle hops.
Seasonals:
   Leinenkugel's Genuine Bock–Brewed since 1888.
  • **Leinenkugel's Big Butt Doppelbock**
  • **Leinenkugel's Berry Weiss**–Flavored with a blend of native Wisconsin loganberries, elderberries, blackberries and honey. Pinkish red color with a strong berry nose. A somewhat sticky sweetness makes this beer reminiscent of a wine cooler.
   Leinenkugel's Autumn Gold
 •• **Leinenkugel's Winter Lager**–A dark lager brewed with six varieties of barley malt, Cascade and Mt. Hood hops. Thin bodied with pleasant roasted malt notes, suggestions of chocolate, and a satisfyingly bitter finish.

BREWERY NOTES
Tours available; call for details. They offer a very nice collection of four different varieties of their beer in a twelve-pack called the "Leinie Lodge Tackle Box."

Dallas, Wisconsin
VIKING BREWING COMPANY

234 Dallas Street, Dallas, WI 54733; phone 715-837-1824
E-mail: results@win.bright.net
Web Address: www.vikingbrewing.com
Type: Microbrewery
Near: 1st Avenue, on the mill pond
Opens: Tours Saturday 1 p.m.
Opening Date: 1994
Most Popular Beer: Copperhead
Brewing System: 5 barrel, customized dairy tanks

BEER LIST
  HoneyMoon
  CopperHead (Oktoberfest)
  Honey Pale Ale–English-style pale brewed with local honey.
  Sylvan Springs Bohemian Lager (Pilsner)
  J. S. Bock (Helles Bock)–Seasonally brewed for Lent each year.
  Root Beer
  Big Swede (Swedish Imperial Stout)
  Abbey Normal (Trappist-style Ale)
  Honeyman Delight–Brewer's interpretation of mead. 8% ABV.

BREWERY NOTES
Located in the historic Dallas Creamery Building on the mill pond. Beer sold to go.

De Pere, Wisconsin
EGAN BREWING COMPANY

330 Reid Street, De Pere, WI 54115
Phone: 920-339-2707 (pub), 920-339-2702 (brewery)
E-mail: gak@beerismylife.com
Type: Microbrewery and Restaurant
Near: Third Street across from St. Norbert College
Nearby City: See Green Bay
Opens: 11 a.m. Monday-Friday; 4 p.m. Saturday-Sunday
Prices: Average
Opening Date: Brewery opened in 1996, restaurant in October 1997
Most Popular Beer: Honey Ale
Brewing System: 3 barrel, DME

BEER LIST
Flagship beers:
- •• **Honey Ale**
- •• **Nut Brown Ale**
- ••• **Pale Ale**–Thin-bodied and citrusy.

Rotating availability:
- •• **Hefeweizen**
- •• **Princess of Darkness Porter**
- • **Raspberry Wheat**
- • **Raspberry Mead**–Honey is substituted for the barley malt.
- •• **Abbot Pennings Belgian Trippel**
- **Irish Stout**–Served via nitrogen tap.
- **Paul's Liberty Pilsener**
- • **Steinworthy Oktoberfest**

BREWERY NOTES
Growlers to go. Their flagship beers, Honey Ale, Nut Brown Ale, and Pale Ale, are all available in bottles under the "Chuck's Famous Ales" label at local Hansen's stores and other retailers.

Delafield, Wisconsin
DELAFIELD BREWHAUS

3832 Hillside Drive, Delafield, WI 53018; phone: 414-646-7821
E-mail: info@delafield-brewhaus.com
Web Address: www.delafield-brewhaus.com
Type: Brewpub
Nearby City: See Milwaukee
Opens: 11 a.m. daily
Opening Date: May 1999

BEER LIST
    Dock Light (Golden Ale)
    Delafield Amber
    Hopfenteufel Alt
    Pewaukee Porter
    Freistadter Pils

Denmark, Wisconsin
GREEN BAY BREWING COMPANY

5312 Steve's Cheese Road, Denmark, WI 54208; phone 920-863-6777
Type: Microbrewery
Nearby City: See Green Bay
Opens: Call for hours
Opening Date: November 1995
Most Popular Beer: Amber Ale and Pale Ale
Brewing System: 30 barrel

BEER LIST
    Hinterland Amber Ale
    Hinterland Pale Ale
    Hinterland Honey Wheat
•••• **Hinterland Maple Bock**–As the name implies this beer is brewed with maple syrup, which provides a subtle yet distinctly maple flavor. Malty sweet with hints of chocolate. Nicely done.
  •• **Packerland Pilsner**–Very easy drinking and refreshing. A good choice for football Sunday.
Seasonals:
  •• **Hinterland Weizen Bier** (Bavarian-style Wheat)–Light bodied and refreshing. Mildly spicy.
    Hinterland Winterland

BREWERY NOTES
Samples available. Call for tour information.

Eagle River, Wisconsin
LOAF & STEIN BREWING COMPANY

219 North Railroad Street, Eagle River, WI 54521; phone 715-477-2739
Web Address: www.bfm.org/loaf&stein
Type: Brewpub
Near: Wall Street
Opens: 11 a.m. Wednesday-Saturday; 9 a.m. Sunday
Prices: Average to expensive
Opening Date: December 1996
Most Popular Beer: Growlin' Bear Nut Brown Ale
Brewing System: 3 barrel, DME

BEER LIST
  Nut Brown Ale
  Wilderness Wheat
  Proud Eagle Pilsner
  Oktoberfest Lager
  Cranberry Bog Fog (Cranberry Wheat)–Unfiltered.
  16 Point Bock (Maibock)
  Yellowbird Pale Ale
  Winter Spiced Ale
  Lumberjack Lager (Dark Lager)
  Growlin' Bear Nut Brown Ale
  Mad Musky Stout
  Railroad Street Porter
  Quinlan Irish Ale

BREWERY NOTES
They also make "Baby J's Root Beer" and "My Cousin's Sarsaparilla" sodas.

Eau Claire, Wisconsin
NORTHWOODS BREWING

3560 Oakwood Mall Drive, Eau Claire, WI 54701; phone 715-552-0511
Type: Brewpub
Near: Golf Road, near the Oakwood Mall
Opens: 11 a.m. daily
Prices: Average
Opening Date: November 1997
Most Popular Beer: Birchwood Pale Ale
Brewing System: 7 barrel, DME

BEER LIST
- **Half Moon Gold**
- **Whitetail Wheat**
- **Birch Wood Ale**
- **Red Cedar Ale**
- **Poplar Porter**
- **Dark Walnut Stout**

BREWERY NOTES
Comfortable lodge atmosphere. Separate bar area with pool table and multiple TVs. Bottled beer is available in six-packs to go.

Egg Harbor, Wisconsin
SHIPWRECKED

7791 Egg Harbor Road, Egg Harbor, WI 54209; phone 920-868-2767
Type: Brewpub
Near: County Road G
Opens: 11 a.m. daily
Prices: Expensive
Opening Date: 1997
Most Popular Beer: Captain's Copper Ale
Brewing System: 15 barrel, Sprinkman

BEER LIST
- **Bayside Blonde Ale**
- **Door County Cherry Wheat**–Made with Door County cherries.
- **Captain's Copper Ale**
- **Peninsula Porter**
- **Lighthouse Light** (American Light Lager)–Brewed with corn.
- **Pumpkin Patch Pumpkin**–Spiced with cinnamon and nutmeg, and brewed with pumpkin.

BREWERY NOTES
Nautical theme. Shipwrecked is also an inn with multiple rooms available. Door County was reportedly a favorite hiding place of Al Capone. It's rumored that an illegitimate son of Al Capone hung himself in the building that now houses the brewery.

Glendale, Wisconsin
SPRECHER BREWING COMPANY

701 W Glendale Avenue, Glendale, WI 53209; phone 414-964-2739
Web Address: www.sprecherbrewery.com
Type: Microbrewery
Near: Highway 43 to Hampton Avenue, one block south to Glendale Avenue.
Nearby City: See Milwaukee
Open: 11 a.m.-6 p.m. Monday-Thursday; 10 a.m.-6 p.m. Friday;
  10 a.m.-5 p.m. Saturday
Opening date: January 1985
Most Popular Beer: Special Amber (flagship beer)
Brewing System: 100 barrel, customized dairy tanks

BEER LIST
Year Round:
•••• **Special Amber** (Vienna-style Lager)–Caramel and hops aroma that nicely predicts the flavor. Very clean. Good hop balance, finishes dry and slightly spicy.
•••• **Black Bavarian** (Schwarzbier)–Kulmbacher-style lager. Nearly black in color. Slightly sour, rich and creamy, with an enormous chocolate finish. Excellent.
•••• **Hefe-Weiss**–Coarse-filtered. Dense, rocky head. Resuspend the sediment before pouring for a beautifully cloudy and tasty beer. Lighter phenolic character than some, but the overall balance of the beer is excellent and very refreshing.
••• **Pub Brown Ale**–Good English ale character in both aroma and flavor. Mildly sweet.
••• **Milwaukee Pilsner**–Dry hopping provides a nice aroma in this well balanced beer. Caramel malt aroma and flavor. Crisp with a dry finish.
Seasonal:
•• **Maibock**
••• **Irish Stout**–Complexly roasty and malty.
   Fest Beer
•••• **Oktoberfest**–Rich caramel nose that skillfully predicts a wonderful malty sweetness, with a flavorful balance provided by Tettnanger hops. Enduring spicy dry finish. An excellent and complex Oktoberfest.
   Winter Brew

(continued)

Sprecher Brewing Company (cont.)

Limited Release:

••• **Russian Imperial Stout**–Seemingly a bit light for an Imperial Stout, but quite enjoyable nonetheless. Rich, silky, and chocolaty sweetness, with fruity components. 8% ABV.

•• **Dopple Bock**–Rich and complex dark lager with obvious alcoholic fortitude. Hints of chocolate. 8% ABV.

India Pale Ale (I.P.A.)–7.5% ABV.

••• **Belgian Ale**–8.5% ABV.

••• **Anniversary Ale**–A Belgian-style brown ale aged with whole raspberries. Good Belgian brown ale character, though a bit on the light side. Nice contribution by the raspberries. Soft and mildly sour, very refreshing.

BREWERY NOTES

Milwaukee's original microbrewery is one of the finest in the Midwest. Sprecher uses gas fired mash and brew kettles that were specially fabricated in-house. Beer sold to go. They also make four gourmet sodas: root beer, Grand Cola, Cream City Cream Soda, and ginger ale. They make all the extracts from scratch in gas-fired kettles.

Green Bay, Wisconsin

For Green Bay breweries, also see these nearby cities: De Pere, Denmark.

Green Bay, Wisconsin
LEGENDS BREWHOUSE AND EATERY
OF GREEN BAY

2840 Shawano Avenue, Green Bay, WI 54313; phone 920-662-1111
Type: Brewpub
Near: Riverview Street
Opens: 11 a.m. daily
Prices: Average
Opening Date: December 1998
Most Popular Beer: Long Tail Light
Brewing System: 4 barrel

BEER LIST
  Long Tail Light
  Duck Creek Dunkel
  Wheat
  Irish Amber

Green Bay, Wisconsin
TITLETOWN BREWING COMPANY

200 Dousman Street, Green Bay, WI 54303; phone 920-437-BEER
Type: Brewpub
Web Address: www.titletownbrewery.com
Near: Broadway Street on the banks of the Fox River near Ray Nitchke
  Memorial Bridge
Opens: 11 a.m. daily
Prices: Average
Opening Date: December 1996
Most Popular Beer: 400 Honey Ale and Railyard Ale
Brewing System: 15 barrel

BEER LIST
- **Grid Iron Gold**
- **400 Honey Ale**
- **Railyard Ale**
- **Johnny "Blood" McNally Irish Red
  Championship Pale Ale**–Made in honor of a Green Bay Packers
  Superbowl victory.
- **Bridge Out Stout**
- **Belgian White Summer Ale**–Traditional Belgian Wit spiced with
  coriander and orange peel.

BREWERY NOTES
Titletown Brewing Company is located in downtown Green Bay in the historic West Side Broadway district. They occupy the old Chicago Northwestern train station built in 1898 on the site of Fort Howard, a fort that once protected the city. The brewery won an award from Governor Thompson and the Wisconsin Main Street Program as the best adaptive reuse of a building. The first floor houses the dining area, while the second floor offers a billiard hall, bar, and a wonderful view of downtown Green Bay and the Fox River. A beer garden is located right along side of the old train tracks. They effectively maintain the atmosphere of an old train station. Growlers, quarter- and half-barrels and to go.

Hartford, Wisconsin
ROTHAUS BREWERY AND RESTAURANT

4900 Highway 175, Hartford, WI 53027; phone 414-644-8181
Type: Brewpub
Near: Located at the intersection of Highway 175 and Highway K
Opens: 4 p.m. daily
Opening Date: October 1998
Brewing System: 7.5 barrel

BREWERY NOTES
All German-style beers

Janesville, Wisconsin
GRAY'S BREWING COMPANY

2424 West Court Street, Janesville, WI 53545; phone 608-754-5150
Web Address: www.graybrewing.com
Type: Microbrewery
Near: West Court Street is also Highway 11 West. The brewery is near the Highway 11 West and Marion Street intersection
Tours: First and third Saturdays of the month at 1:30 p.m.
Opening Date: 1856 originally, restarted beer operations in 1994
Most Popular Beer: Gray's Honey Ale
Brewing System: 27 barrel

BEER LIST
- ••• **Classic American Pale Ale**–Soft and lightly malty body, gently balanced with a subtle hop finish. Easy drinking American ale.
- • **Black and Tan**–More tan than black. Lightly malty.
- ••• **Classic Oatmeal Stout**–Subtle molasses-like sweetness with a bit of roastiness and burnt malt bitterness.
- • **Wisconsin Weissbier** (Bavarian-style Wheat)
- •• **Gray's Honey Ale**–Brewed with 100% Wisconsin honey. Rather light and easy drinking with a subdued honey sweetness.
  Wassail Ale–A spiced seasonal.
  Gray's Cream Ale
  Gray's Irish Ale
  Gray's Autumn Ale (Nut Brown Ale)
  Gray's Winter Porter (Robust Porter)

BREWERY NOTES
Gray's Brewing and Beverage Company is reportedly the nation's oldest family owned beverage company, maintaining continuous business for over 138 years. In 1912 Gray's discontinued brewing operations and produced only soft drinks until 1994, when they again fired up the brewery. They now produce over 10,000 barrels of beer annually. Gray's also offers four soft drinks available year round: root beer, cream soda, strawberry, and orange.

Junction City, Wisconsin
CENTRAL WATERS BREWING

701 Main Street (Highway 10), Junction City WI 54443
Phone: 715-457-3322
E-mail: mac@tznet.com
Web Address: www.coredcs.com/~rborowit/brewery/brewery.htm
Type: Microbrewery
Near: Just west of the railroad track in downtown Junction City
Opens: Hours by appointment
Opening Date: January 1997
Most Popular Beer: Mud Puppy Porter
Brewing System: 7.5 barrel, customized dairy tanks

BEER LIST
Year Round:
  Happy Heron Pale Ale (American-style Pale Ale)
  Ouisconsing Red–Named after the Native American word for the
    Wisconsin River.
  Mud Puppy Porter
Seasonals:
  Whitewater Weizen (Bavarian-style Wheat) – Unfiltered.
  Old Bog and Paddy Ale–Brewed with cranberry and wild rice.
  Satin Solstice Imperial Stout–Described by the brewery as "high
    octane."

BREWERY NOTES
Housed in a renovated Model A dealership that has been a multitude of businesses over the years.

As of late 1998 they were scheduled to have begun bottling in 22-ounce and 1 liter snap caps. Beers are available on tap locally and in quarter- and half-barrels

Kenosha, Wisconsin
BREWMASTERS PUB AND RESTAURANT

4017 80th Street, Kenosha, WI 53142; phone 414-694-9050
Type: Brewpub
Near: 39th Avenue
Opens: 11 a.m. daily
Prices: Average to expensive
Opening Date: February 1987
Most Popular Beer: Kenosha Gold
Brewing System: 7 barrel

BEER LIST
> Icemaster–Brewed with corn as an adjunct.
- **Kenosha Gold** (Pilsner)
- **Southport Amber**
- **Saint Brendan's Oatmeal Stout**
- **Oktoberfest**

Kenosha, Wisconsin
BREWMASTERS PUB PARKSIDE

1170 22nd Avenue, Kenosha, WI 53142; phone 414-552-2805
Type: Brewpub
Opens: 11 a.m. daily
Opening Date: May 1997
Most Popular Beer: Kenosha Gold
Brewing System: 15 barrel

BEER LIST & BREWERY NOTES
See Brewmasters Pub and Restaurant, also in Kenosha. They brew the same basic recipes, but with different specialty beers.

La Crosse, Wisconsin
BODEGA BREWPUB

122 South 4th Street, La Crosse, WI 54601; phone 608-782-0677
Type: Brewpub
Near: Between Pearl and Main streets
Opens: Noon daily

BEER LIST & BREWERY NOTES
Large imported bottled beer list and several Wisconsin brewed beers on tap. Their own brewing is in very small batches and availability is irregular; in fact, none of their beers were available at the time of my visit in October 1998.

Homebrew supplies available.

La Crosse, Wisconsin
BLACK ROSE BREWHAUS

300 South 3rd Street, La Crosse, WI 54601; phone 608-796-BEER
Type: Brewpub
Near: Jay Street
Opens: 11 a.m. daily

BEER LIST & BREWERY NOTES
German-style restaurant, complete with wiener schnitzel. Scheduled to start brewing their own beer sometime in 1999.

La Crosse, Wisconsin
DOC POWELL'S POTIONS, PROVISIONS AND PUBERY

200 Main Street, La Crosse, WI 54601; phone 608-785-7026
Type: Brewpub
Near: 2nd and Main streets in the historic Powell Place Mall
Opens: 11:30 a.m. Monday-Saturday; closed Sunday
Prices: Average to expensive
Opening Date: May 1998
Most Popular Beer: Paddle Wheel Pale Ale

BEER LIST
- •• **Kickapoo Blonde**
- •• **Cat Whisker Wheat** (Bavarian-style Wheat)–Unfiltered.
- •• **Paddle Wheel Pale Ale**
- • **Mighty Miss Red Ale**
- •• **Grand Dad's Stout**–Nice chocolate malt aroma. Subtle complexities including roasty and mild smoky characteristics.

BREWERY NOTES
At the time of my visit (October 1998) the beers were being made by a sister brewery in South Dakota (Sioux Falls Brewing Company). They plan to brew their own beers in 1999. All beers are well made, tending toward the light end of the spectrum. A selection of single malt Scotch is available.

They are the only brewery I am aware of that offers an emu burger. Emu are similar to ostriches.

Lake Delton, Wisconsin
PUMPHOUSE PIZZA AND BREWERY

19 West Monroe Avenue, Lake Delton, WI 53940; phone 608-253-4687
Type: Brewpub
Near: Corner of Highways 12 and 23
Opens: 11 a.m. daily
Prices: Average
Opening Date: Brewing since June 1998
Brewing System: 90 gallon

BEER LIST
    American Pilsner
- **Dark Wheat**
- **Great Wisconsin Dells Summer Wheat**

BREWERY NOTES
Unique, fun atmosphere. Gas station theme with pumps outside and a slew of service station decorations inside. Some of the staff even wear service station uniforms. Fifty domestic and imported bottled beers. Pool table and darts.

Madison, Wisconsin
For Madison Breweries, also see Middleton.

Madison, Wisconsin
ANGELIC BREWING COMPANY

322 West Johnson, Madison, WI 53703; phone 608-257-2707
E-mail: twrsang@aol.com
Web Address: www.angelicbrewing.com
Type: Brewpub
Near: Broom Street
Opens: 3 p.m. Monday-Wednesday; 11 a.m. Thursday-Sunday
Prices: Average
Opening Date: February 1995
Most Popular Beer: Bacchanal Blonde
Brewing System: 15 barrel

BEER LIST
    Believers Bitter
    Bacchanal Blonde (Golden Ale)
- • **Harvest Moon Hefe-Weizen**
    Raspberry Wheat
- **Shakedown Nut Brown**
    Sinners Stout

PUB & BREWING CO.

Madison, Wisconsin
GREAT DANE PUB &
BREWING COMPANY

123 East Doty Street, Madison, WI 53703
Phone: 608-284-0000
E-mail: gdanebrew@mailbag.com
Web Address: www.greatdanepub.com
Type: Brewpub
Opens: 11 a.m. daily
Prices: Average
Opening Date: November 1994
Most Popular Beer: Pilsner, Red, Scotch Ale and Porter
Brewing System: 10 barrel

BEER LIST

••• **Landmark Gold**–Good flavor and nice bitter finish, but not too challenging for the uninitiated.

••• **Peck's Pilsner**

•••• **Crop Circle Wheat**–Unfiltered. 60% wheat malt, imported German ingredients. Rich and spicy.

•••• **Old Glory American Pale Ale**–Cascade hops are added at 5 different times during the brewing. Wonderful citrus hop character that is complex and slightly resinous.

• **Bank Shot Nut Brown Ale**

••• **Devil's Lake Red Lager**–Creamy soft head, very easy drinking.

••• **Stone of Scone Scotch Ale**

•• **Emerald Isle Stout**

•••• **Black Earth Porter**–Silky and malty sweet porter with chocolate and coffee notes. Strong roasty bitterness. Nine varieties of malt are used.

•••• **Potters Run I.P.A.**–Hopped assertively with Goldings. A touch of alcohol in the flavor.

•• **Kölsch**

•• **Blackwolf**–Named for Madison's minor league baseball team and sold at the ballpark.

•• **Drop Anchor Steam** (California Common)–Hmm . . . I wonder what beer this is patterned after?

•• **Oktoberfest**–Light caramel malt character.

••• **Belgian Wit**–Flavored with coriander and orange peel.

(continued)

Great Dane Pub & Brewing Company (cont.)

•• **John Jacob Jingleheimer Schmidt's Dunkel Doppel Hefe-Weizen Bock**–An obvious winner for longest beer name ever. At least I hope it is. As you might guess, it's dark, strong and sweet, unfiltered, cloudy, and phenolic.

BREWERY NOTES
Excellent food and beer. Great Dane routinely offers 10 to 14 beers on tap; more importantly and impressively, each is an accurate interpretation of the style it represents. They have a huge beer garden in back, and have recently added a small pool hall and cigar smoking area. Live bands Thursday and Sunday.

Madison, Wisconsin
JT WHITNEY'S BREWPUB AND EATERY

674 South Whitney Way, Madison, WI 53711; phone 608-274-1776
E-mail: Brewery@jtwhitneys.com
Web Address: www.jtwhitneys.com
Type: Brewpub
Near: 1 block north of the Beltline on Whitney Way
Opens: 11:00 a.m. daily
Opening Date: Opened October 1995. First beer brewed February 1996.
Most Popular Beer: Badger Red Ale
Brewing System: 10 barrel, DME

BEER LIST
    Goldenshine (Light Golden Ale)
    J.T.'s Badger Red Ale (Irish-style Red Ale)
    Black Diamond Porter.
    Heartland Weiss (Bavarian-style Wheat)–70% wheat malt.
    Willy Street Weizenbock (Bavarian-style Wheat Bock)
    Pinckney Street Pale Ale–Unfiltered, Cascade hops.
    Stonehenge Stout (Irish Stout)
    State Street Stout
    I.P.A.
    Traditional Irish Ale
    Rich's Rauch (Smoked Ale)

BREWERY NOTES
Beers are available at bars and restaurants on a limited basis through a local distributor. Many seasonal beers. They also offer special events such as cigar dinners, beer schools, bourbon and Scotch tastings, and more.

Marinette, Wisconsin
RAILHOUSE RESTAURANT AND BREWERY

2029 Old Peshtigo Road, Marinette, WI 54143; phone 715-735-9800
Type: Brewpub
Near: Highway 41 and Cleveland Avenue
Opens: 10 a.m. daily
Prices: Average
Opening Date: July 1995
Most Popular Beer: Silver Steam and Railhouse Red
Brewing System: 2 barrel

BEER LIST
- **Rail House Silver** (Pale Ale)
- **Rail House Pilsner**
- **Rail House Honey**
- **Rail House Gold Rush** (California Common)
- **Rail House Red**
  Rail House Stout

BREWERY NOTES
A railroad theme on property that used to house railroad personnel. During prohibition it was used as a house of ill repute. Arcade and pinball games are available.

Middleton, Wisconsin
CAPITAL BREWING COMPANY

7734 Terrace Avenue, Middleton, WI 53562
Phone: 608-836-7100
Web Address: www.capital-brewery.com

Type: Microbrewery
Nearby City: Madison
Opens: Hours vary seasonally; call first
Opening Date: Spring 1986
Most Popular Beer: Wisconsin Amber
Brewing System: 35.5 barrel, 1955 German Hupmen Brewhouse

BEER LIST
Year Round:
•••• **Bavarian Lager**–A very fresh and light malt/hop nose, soft body.
•••• **Special Pilsner**–Soft, malty body, nicely hopped, finishing mildly salty.
••• **Munich Dark**
•• **Wisconsin Amber**–Nice dry finish.
　　Kloster Weizen
　　Raspberry Wheat
•••• **Capital Brown Ale**–Lightly malty with no obvious hop bitterness. A very nice interpretation of the style.
Seasonals:
　　Bock
　　Maibock
•• **Fest**
　　Oktoberfest
　　Wild Rice
　　Winterfest
　　Doppelbock

BREWERY NOTES
Located in a building that formerly housed an egg processing plant and cold storage for poultry products. The site is now being put to much better use. Their Pilsner and Bavarian lager are among only a handful of truly authentic tasting German lagers brewed in the Midwest. They market their beer under the brand name Garten Bräu. As one would expect from a brewery producing excellent German-style beers, they brew in strict accordance with the Reinheitsgebot, with the exception of their Raspberry Wheat and Wild Rice

(continued)

158

Capital Brewing Company (cont.)

beers. From late May through late September, they serve beer in their beer garden on Thursday and Friday evenings and Saturday afternoon and evenings. Peanuts are available as a snack. Beer is sold to go.

Milwaukee, Wisconsin

For Milwaukee breweries, also see these nearby cities: Delafield, Glendale, Waukesha

Milwaukee, Wisconsin
LAKEFRONT BREWERY

1872 North Commerce Street, Milwaukee, WI 53212
Phone: 414-372-8800
E-mail: lakefront@execpc.com
Web Address: www.lakefront-brewery.com
Type: Microbrewery
Near: Humbolt and Locust streets, near Tracks Tavern
Open: 8 a.m.-5 p.m. weekdays. Call for Saturday hours.
Opening Date: December 1987
Most Popular Beer: Riverwest Stein Beer
Brewing System: 6 barrel

BEER LIST

- ••• **Cream City Pale Ale**–Named for the cream-colored brick buildings that earned Milwaukee the name Cream City. Spicy dry finish.
- • **Extra Special Organic Bitter** (E.S.B.)– Made with all organic malts, OCIA Certified Organic Ale.
- •• **Klisch Pilsner**–Hoppy with a dry finish.
- •••• **East Side Dark**–Excellent dark lager, a bit on the strong side. Rich malty character, some alcohol contributions, and a mellow chocolaty finish. Nearly a bock.
- ••• **Riverwest Stein Beer** (Vienna Lager)–Medium malty body with a dry and slightly spicy finish.
- •• **Pumpkin Lager Beer**–Intensely spicy aroma and flavor. Spicy dry finish.
- • **Fuel Coffee Stout**
  Bock
  Cherry
  Spice–Brewed with cinnamon, cloves, ginger, orange peel, and honey.

BREWERY NOTES

Located in a historic building that formerly was a bakery. Brewery tours given Friday at 5:30 p.m., and Saturday at 1:30, 2:30, and 3:30. Voted "Best Brewery Tour" by *Milwaukee Magazine.*

All beers are unfiltered. Their Pumpkin Lager was voted "Best Seasonal Beer" by *Milwaukee Magazine.*

Milwaukee, Wisconsin
MILWAUKEE ALE HOUSE

233 North Water Street, Milwaukee, WI 53202; phone 414-226-2337
E-mail: mike@ale-house.com
Web Address: www.ale-house.com
Type: Brewpub
Near: Between Buffalo and Chicago Street
Opens: 11 a.m. daily
Prices: Average
Opening Date: 1987
Most Popular Beer: Downtown Lites (Honey Ale)
Brewing System: 15 barrel, Sprinkman

BEER LIST
  Downtown Lites (Honey Ale)
  Session Ale (Mild Ale)–3% ABV.
  Pullchain Pail Ale (American-style Pale Ale)
  Solomon Juneau Ale–Saaz hops.
  Louie's Demise Ale
  Sheepshead Stout

BREWERY NOTES
In the historic "Third Ward" area of Milwaukee.

Milwaukee, Wisconsin
ROCK BOTTOM BREWERY

740 North Plankinton, Milwaukee, WI 53203; phone 414-276-3030
Web Address: www.rockbottom.com
Type: Brewpub
Near: Corner of Wells and Plankinton in downtown Milwaukee on the river
Opens: 11 a.m daily
Prices: Average to expensive
Opening Date: March 1997
Most Popular Beers: Greenfield, Honey Creek, and Raccoon Red
Brewing System: 12 barrel, J.V. Northwest

BEER LIST
- **Greenfield American Light** (Blonde Ale)
- **Honeycreek Pale Ale**–Cascade hops.
- **Raccoon Red**–Nugget, Willamette and Cascade hops.
- **Brown Bear Brown**
- **Stillwater Stout**

BREWERY NOTES
Outdoor seating overlooking the river. Large Colorado-based brewpub chain with many locations. Twelve or more specialty beers every year that vary seasonally. Generally 7-8 beers on tap at any one time.

Rock Bottom incorporates their beers into a number of menu items, including a carrot cake made with a touch of their pale ale.

Milwaukee, Wisconsin
WATER STREET BREWERY

1101 North Water Street, Milwaukee, WI 53202; phone 414-272-1195
Web Address: www.restaurantour.com/wsb/
Type: Brewpub
Near: East Highland Street
Opens: 11 a.m. daily
Prices: Average
Opening Date: 1987
Most Popular Beer: Honey Lager Light
Brewing System: 7 barrel

BEER LIST
  Pilsner
  Weiss (Bavarian-style Wheat)
  Pale Ale
  Amber
  Oktoberfest

Mineral Point, Wisconsin
BREWERY CREEK BREWING

23 Commerce Street, Mineral Point, WI 53565; phone 608-987-3298
E-mail: brewpub@mhtc.net
Web Address: www.brewerycreek.com
Type: Brewpub
Near: 2 blocks from High Street
Opens: 11 a.m. daily
Prices: Average
Opening Date: July 1998
Brewing System: 15 barrel

BEER LIST
••• **German Ale**–Copper colored beer. Fresh caramel malt sweetness
    initially with balancing hop bitterness in the finish.
•• **Mahogany Ale**

BREWERY NOTES
Mineral Point, once known for its lead mines, is a small touristy town with a
number of antique shops. The brewpub itself is uniquely decorated with a
weathered-looking exposed wood beam ceiling and many interesting dining
tables, no two alike.

Brewery Creek Brewing offers a very cozy European pub atmosphere, and
in the European tradition, the brewery offers an inn upstairs. All rooms have
cable TV, air conditioning, and private phones. A continental breakfast is
offered for guests. Rooms start at $125 per night.

Minocqua, Wisconsin
MINOCQUA BREWING

238 Lake Shore Drive, Minocqua, WI 54548; phone 715-358-3040
Type: Brewpub
Near: Oneida, just off south Highway 51
Opens: 11 a.m. daily
Prices: Average
Opening Date: 1997
Most Popular Beer: Brewmaster Special
Brewing System: 7 barrel, A& B Process Systems

BEER LIST

- ••• **Island City Pale Ale** (American-style Pale Ale)–Nice Cascade kick in both flavor and bitterness. Thin bodied and refreshing.
  Northern Blonde
- •• **330 Red Ale**–Named after the building they occupy, the Masonic Lodge 330. Mild caramel malt sweetness.
- •••• **Pitsaw Porter**–Brewed with both chocolate malt and rye. Rich chocolaty sweetness. The touch of rye offers an interesting balance. A skillfully made and atypical porter.
- ••• **7 Malt and Wild Rice** (a rotating special)–An interesting, unique beer. Very grainy with a touch of astringency and a nice bitter finish.

BREWERY NOTES
Attractive lodge setting. Ask for seating in the back for a gorgeous view of the lake. Definitely worth a detour if you are traveling nearby.

Monroe, Wisconsin
JOSEPH HUBER BREWING COMPANY

1208 14th Street, Monroe, WI 53566; phone 608-325-3191
Type: Regional Brewery
Opens: No brewery tours available
Opening Date: 1845
Most Popular Beer: Berghoff Original Lager Beer
Brewing System: 375 barrel

BEER LIST
- •• **Berghoff Original Lager Beer**–Surprisingly hoppy and perfumy. Soft malty balance, slightly astringent.
- ••• **Berghoff Famous Bock Beer**–Mildly sweet with hints of chocolate. Subtle alcohol nose and flavor. A highly drinkable and enjoyable bock.
- ••• **Genuine Dark Beer**–Hints of chocolate, medium bodied and sweet.
- •• **Oktober Fest Beer**–Copper colored lager with a spicy hop nose and finish.
- •• **Berghoff Honey Maibock**–Predominant honey character.
  Berghoff Hazelnut Fest Ale
- •• **Famous Red Ale**–Caramel finish.

BREWERY NOTES
Joseph Huber Brewing is the oldest brewery in the Midwest. They survived prohibition by producing root beer and ginger beer, and today have a brewing capacity of 150,000 barrels per year. Their brands, which can be found all over Wisconsin, include Berghoff, Huber, Wisconsin Club, and Rhinelander.

Mount Horeb, Wisconsin
MOUNT HOREB PUB AND BREWERY

105 South Second Street, Mount Horeb, WI 53572; phone 608-437-4200
Type: Brewpub
Near: Main Street
Opens: 11 a.m. Monday-Friday; 11:30 a.m. Saturday-Sunday
Prices: Average
Opening Date: October 1998
Most Popular Beer: Trailside Wheat
Brewing System: 10 barrel, steam-fired DME

BEER LIST
Trollway Lager–Mount Horeb has a number of intriguing Troll statues along Main Street, which is called the "Trollway."
Trailside Wheat (Bavarian-style Wheat)
How Now Brown Cow (Brown Ale)
Liberty Pole Ale (American-style Pale Ale)–Cascade hops.
Valhalla Stout (Dry Stout)
Spiced Porter

BREWERY NOTES
Only one block away from the Mount Horeb Mustard Museum. Yes, that's right, a mustard museum.

Mukwonago, Wisconsin
JK SILVER BREWING

621 Baxter Drive, Mukwonago WI 53149; phone 414-363-9359
Type: Microbrewery
Opening Date: March 1996

BEER LIST
• **Amber Ale**

New Glarus
Brewing Co.

New Glarus, Wisconsin
NEW GLARUS BREWING COMPANY

County Road W and Highway 69, New Glarus, WI 53574
Phone: 608-527-5850
Type: Microbrewery

Near: Highway 69
Open: Noon-4:30 p.m. Monday-Saturday. Tours available Saturdays at 1,
2, 3, and 4 p.m.
Opening Date: October 1993
Most Popular Beer: Edel Pils
Brewing System: 100 barrel copper system

BEER LIST
Edel Pils
- •• **Uff-da Bock**–Malty, with significant alcohol character and hints of chocolate. 7.3% ABV.
- •••• **Apple Ale**–Made with four varieties of Wisconsin apples. The result is a wonderfully flavorful hybrid of cider and beer. 3.8% ABV.
- •••• **Belgian Red Brand Wisconsin Cherry Ale** (Fruit/Lambic)–Over a pound of Wisconsin grown cherries go into each bottle of this absolutely fantastic and unique beer. Brewed with hops aged for a year, Wisconsin farmed wheat, Belgian roasted barleys, and conditioned in oak tanks. An outstanding interpretation of this delicious Belgian style. 5% ABV.
- •••• **Raspberry Tart** (Fruit/Lambic)–A Wisconsin framboise. Deep burgundy colored. Brewed with Wisconsin farmed wheat, Oregon berries, and year old Hallertau hops. Unbelievably fresh and intense raspberry nose, reminiscent of fresh raspberry pie. It starts quite sweet, but quickly turns decidedly tart. This is yet another wonderful blend of beer and fruit.
  Coffee Stout
  Norski Honey Bock (Maibock) –7.8% ABV.
- ••• **Dan's Best Bitter**–British Otter Pale Malt and East Kent Golding hops. Lightly carbonated, caramel malt flavor with an assertive hop balance.
  Solstice (Bavarian-style Wheat)
  Staghorn (Oktoberfest)
  Snowshoe (Amber Ale)
- •• **Zwickel** (Wisconsin lager with yeast)–Unfiltered and bottle conditioned lager. An interesting beer and an unusual style.

(continued)

166

New Glarus Brewing Company (cont.)
BREWERY NOTES
Tours available with beer samples. Beer sold to go. Winner of numerous awards including "Wisconsin's Best Brewery" by *Wisconsin Trails Magazine*, and "1995's Top Ten Breweries in the World" by *World Brewery Championships*.

I keep a private stock of both the Raspberry Tart and Wisconsin Cherry at home. I cherish them while they last, and consider it a personal tragedy when they are gone. These beers are simply fantastic, and are both on my short list of the finest beers made in the United States. They are not only fine examples of a Belgian-style beer, but they also have their own unique flair and character.

Oconomowoc, Wisconsin
OCONOMOWOC BREWING
750 East Wisconsin, Oconomowoc, WI 53066; phone 414-560-0388
Type: Microbrewery
Near: Near Highway 67 bypass
Opens: Variable hours
Opening Date: Late 1998
Brewing System: 35 barrel, customized dairy tanks

BEER LIST
   Alt
   Amber Rye Lager

BREWERY NOTES
Initially they will be supplying keg accounts only.

Oshkosh, Wisconsin
FRATELLO'S AND FOX RIVER BREWING COMPANY

1501 Arboretum Drive, Oshkosh, WI 54901; phone 414-232-2337
E-mail: info@foxriverbrewing.com
Web Address: www.foxriverbrewing.com
Type: Brewpub
Near: Highway 23 east/Oshkosh Avenue bridge
Opens: 11 a.m. daily
Opening Date: December 1995
Most Popular Beer: Winnebago Wheat and Caber Tossing Scottish Ale
Brewing System: 10 barrel

BEER LIST & BREWERY NOTES
Live music on the patio during the summer. See listing for the Appleton Fox River location.

Port Washington, Wisconsin
HARBOR CITY BREWING COMPANY

535 West Grand Avenue, Port Washington, WI 53074
Phone: 414-284-3118
Web Address: www.execpc.com/~oldcat/hcbindx.htm
Type: Microbrewery
Open: Tours available noon-4 p.m. on Saturdays
Opening Date: June 1997
Most Popular Beer: Mile Rock Amber Ale
Brewing System: 20 barrel

BEER LIST
- **Mile Rock Amber Ale**
- ••• **Main Street Brown Ale**–Described as a robust brown ale. Perhaps a bit heavy for a brown, but I found it very enjoyable. Soft and malty with a chocolaty finish and very little hop bitterness.
- ••• **Transcendental Wheat Beer**–Belgian wheat malt. A subtle addition of orange blossom honey and orange peel mingle nicely in this refreshing beer.

BREWERY NOTES
Housed in a former ice plant. The brewery worked closely with New Belgium Brewing Company of Fort Collins, Colorado (creators of Fat Tire Amber Ale), in designing their facility. Beer available to go.

Port Washington, Wisconsin
PORT WASHINGTON BREWING

100 North Franklin Avenue, Port Washington WI 53074
Phone: 414-377-BEER
Type: Brewpub
Opens: 11 a.m. daily
Prices: Expensive
Opening Date: July 1996
Most Popular Beer: Pier 96 Lager
Brewing System: 10 barrel, fully automated Sprinkman

BEER LIST
- **Raspberry Wheat**
- **Hefe-Weizen**
- **Pier 96 Lager** (American Light Lager)
- **Amber**
- **• Port Porter**

BREWERY NOTES
Located in the same building as the Fish Shanty restaurant and the Schooner pub. Upscale restaurant with a nautical theme. Seating available with a view of Lake Michigan.

Reedsburg, Wisconsin
ENDEHOUSE BREWERY AND RESTAURANT

1020 East Main Street, Reedsburg, WI 53959; phone 608-524-8600
Type: Brewpub
Opens: 4 p.m. daily
Prices: Average
Opening Date: August 1997
Most Popular Beer: Old Gold and Black Beauty
Brewing System: 2 barrel

BEER LIST
   Old Gold (German-style Pilsner)
   Pale Ale
•• **Black Beauty** (Porter)–Silky and sweet.
   Dunkel Weiss
   Gold Ribbon (Amber Lager)
 • **Dave's I.P.A.**
•• **Dry Stout**
 • **Oktoberfest**–Hallertau, Spalt, and Tettnang hops.
 • **Bootlegger Lager**–Brewed for the Sesquicentennial.
••• **Weiss**–Dense foam head, good wheat sourness.

BREWERY NOTES
A house converted into a restaurant and brewery.

Rhinelander, Wisconsin
BROWN STREET BREWERY AND
BUGSY'S SPORTS BAR

16 North Brown Street, Rhinelander, WI 54501; phone 715-369-2100
Type: Brewpub
Opens: 11 a.m. Monday-Friday; 10 a.m. Saturday and Sunday
Opening Date: 1998
Most Popular Beer: Munich

BEER LIST
   Czechoslovakian Pilsner
   Stout
   Munich
   Amber

BREWERY NOTES
Many pool tables are available. Big screen TVs. They even have a half basketball court for kids.

Stevens Point, Wisconsin
STEVENS POINT BREWERY

2617 Water Street, Stevens Point, WI 54481; phone 800-369-4911
Web Address: www.pointbeer.com
Type: Regional Brewery
Opens: Hours vary seasonally
Opening Date: 1857
Most Popular Beer: Stevens Point Special
Brewing System: 200 barrel

BEER LIST
Year Round:
••• **Stevens Point Special** (American Lager)–Their flagship brand since
    1857. Refreshing lager with a subtle maltiness and an extremely light
    hop component.
 • **Point Pale Ale**–Cascade and Williamette hops. Introduced in 1995.
 •• **Point Classic Amber**–Introduced in 1994. Lightly spicy.
    Point Maple Wheat
    Point Light
Seasonals:
••• **Point Bock**–Introduced in 1938. A light, strongly caramel-like bock.
    Point Winter Spice

BREWERY NOTES
Call for information on brewery tour times

Sturgeon Bay, Wisconsin
STURGEON BAY BREWING

341-C North Third Avenue, Sturgeon Bay WI 54235
Phone: 920-746-7611
Type: Brewpub
Near: Jefferson and Third Avenue
Opens: 10 a.m. daily
Prices: Average to expensive
Opening Date: February 1998
Brewing System: 10 barrel

BEER LIST
 • **Amber Ale**
   Pumpkin
   Helles

BREWERY NOTES
2.5-gallon party pigs to go. They bought their brewing equipment from
Cherryland Brewing. In fact, as of October 1998, they were still selling
bottled Cherryland beers at their pub.

Waukesha, Wisconsin
REMINGTON WATSON SMITH
BREWING COMPANY

223 Maple Avenue, Waukesha, WI 53186; phone 414-896-7766
Type: Microbrewery
Nearby City: See Milwaukee
Opens: Hours variable
Opening Date: 1994
Most Popular Beer: Amber Ale
Brewing System: 6.5 barrel, customized dairy tanks

BEER LIST
Year Round:
  Old Waukesha Pale Ale
  Watsons Amber ale
  Brown Ale
  Lake Country Lager
Seasonals:
  Oktoberfest
  Nocturne Ale–High gravity dark ale.
  Blond Bock
  Rye Beer

Whitewater, Wisconsin
RANDY'S RESTAURANT & FUN HUNTER'S
BREWERY

841 East Milwaukee Street, Whitewater, WI 53190; phone 414-473-8000
E-mail: rcruse@mail.idcnet.com
Type: Brewpub
Near: U.S. Highway 12 (Milwaukee Street) and Willard
Opens: 11 a.m. on Tuesday-Thursday and Saturday; 10:30 a.m. on Sunday
Prices: Expensive
Opening Date: Started brewing in 1994
Most Popular Beer: Amber Lager

BEER LIST
Amber Lager
  •• **Wheat Ale**
  • **Pre-Prohibition Lager**
  •• **Oatmeal Stout**
  •• **Golden Pilsner**
  • **Oktoberfest**

BREWERY NOTES
Clubhouse atmosphere with a separate sports bar area.

BEER STYLE GUIDE

$\mathcal{T}$his section provides a starting point for understanding and appreciating some of the style diversity that is now available in the Great Lakes region. Where applicable, I have included recommended Great Lakes brewed examples of each style of beer.

This is by no means a comprehensive look at the complex world of beer. Entire books have been written on beer styles, and they are available at most bookstores. I especially recommend the *Classic Beer Style Series,* published by Brewers Publications, Inc. Each book focuses on a specific style of beer.

Ales
American and English Style Ales

Generally, American ales are stronger, bigger bodied, and more aggressively hopped than their British counterparts. American and British style ales are the most frequently brewed beer styles in American microbreweries.

American Amber Ale
Usually medium-bodied beers with a noticeable maltiness and often a somewhat assertive hop character from American hop varieties.

Most finish spicy and dry. Ale fruitiness ranges from absent to moderate.

Recommended Great Lakes examples: Abana Amber Ale (Mickey Finn's Brewery, Illinois), Bell's Amber (Kalamazoo Brewing, Michigan).

American Blonde/Golden Ale

Often a light variation of the American pale ale. Straw-golden colored, usually crisp and dry with a light body and flavor. Frequently used as a "training-wheels" beer to help consumers move from American light lagers to more full-flavored beers.

Recommended Great Lakes examples: Big Ben House Mild (Arbor Brewing, Michigan); Buckeye Boys Blonde (Maumee Bay Brewing, Ohio); Freestone Blonde (Bloomington Brewing, Indiana); Gold (Michigan Brewing, Michigan); Landmark Gold (Great Dane Pub & Brewing, Wisconsin); Sandstone Light (Lake Superior Brewing, Michigan); Searchlight Golden Ale (Alcatraz Brewing, Indiana); Very Pale Ale (Taylor Brewing, Illinois), Blond Ale (Goose Island Beer Co., Illinois).

American Pale Ale

Usually a copper colored beer. This style can vary widely. Some examples are balanced with a malty body and moderate hop bitterness, while others can be quite assertive in both hop flavor and bitterness. Typically, American pale ales are less malty than British varieties, and place more emphasis on hop flavor and bitterness. Alcohol contents are usually around 4.5-5.5% ABV. Fruity ester flavors can range from mild to strong. The style is a proving ground for aromatic American hop varieties, Cascade hops being one of the most common. *Classic Example:* Sierra Nevada Pale Ale

Recommended Great Lakes examples: Alpha King Pale Ale, X-tra Pale Ale (Three Floyds Brewing, Indiana); Anchor Bay Pale Ale (North Channel Brewing, Michigan); Bell's Pale Ale (Kalamazoo Brewing, Michigan); Black Diamond Pale Ale (Diamondback Brewery, Ohio); Burning River Pale Ale (Great Lakes Brewing, Ohio);

Cream City Pale Ale (Lakefront Brewery, Wisconsin); Forecaster Pale Ale (Roffey Brewing, Michigan); Honker's Ale (Goose Island Brewing, Illinois); Island City Pale Ale (Minocqua Brewing, Wisconsin); Old Glory American Pale Ale (Great Dane Pub & Brewing, Wisconsin); Paddy Pale Ale (Wild Onion Brewing, Illinois); Pale Ale (Michigan Brewing, Michigan); Petoskey Stone Pale Ale (Bear River Brewing, Michigan); Prophet's Rock Pale Ale (Lafayette Brewing, Indiana); Quarrymen Pale Ale (Bloomington Brewing, Indiana); Red Snapper Special Bitter (Arbor Brewing, Michigan); Rev. Purley Pale Ale (Hoster Brewing, Ohio); Sandstone Pale Ale (Lake Superior Brewing, Michigan); Tornado Pale Ale (Olde Peninsula Brewpub & Restaurant, Michigan).

American Wheat
American wheat beers are fermented with regular ale yeast. Thus, they do not exhibit the phenolic spiciness or unique fruitiness of their Bavarian counterparts. This style is generally brewed with upwards of 50 percent wheat malt. These beers have light and crisp grainy flavors, are lightly hopped, and often exhibit a refreshing sourness. Quenching and unchallenging to the novice beer drinker, American wheat beers have become extremely popular in brewpubs throughout the Midwest. Commonly combined with raspberries, cherries, or some other fruit. Also available in dark varieties. *Recommended Great Lakes examples:* Bell's Oberon (Kalamazoo Brewing, Michigan) Dark Wheat Ale (Alcatraz Brewing, Indiana); Razz Wheat (Oaken Barrel Brewing, Indiana); Rockin' Raspberry Wheat (Olde Peninsula Brewpub & Restaurant, Michigan); Scarlett's Raspberry Wheat (Founders Hill Brewing, Illinois); Wheat Wave Ale (Roffey Brewing, Michigan).

Brown Ale
The style comes in three varieties. *English Mild Ale* ranges in color from amber to dark brown, is lightly malty, low in hop bitterness and alcohol, and may exhibit a light nuttiness. The emphasis is on a light bodied maltiness. *English Brown Ale* is stronger, displaying

175

similar characteristics. *American Brown Ale* can be stronger still with an increased hop aroma and bitterness. Due to the mild nature of this style, brown ales are easily quaffed and often successfully used to introduce beer novices to the world of dark beer. *Classic examples:* Newcastle Brown Ale, Samuel Smith's Nut Brown Ale, and Pete's Wicked Ale.

Recommended Great Lakes examples: 2 Penny Wee Mild (Lafayette Brewing, Indiana); Bell's Best Brown (Kalamazoo Brewing, Michigan); Bevo Brown Ale (Wild Onion Brewing, Illinois); Big Daddy Brown (Mad Anthony's Brewing, Indiana); Brown Ale (Michigan Brewing, Michigan); Brown Ale (Two Brothers Brewing, Illinois); Capital Brown Ale (Capital Brewing, Wisconsin); Crown Brown Ale (King Brewing, Michigan); Granite Brown (Lake Superior Brewing, Michigan); Hexnut Brown Ale (Goose Island Brewing, Illinois); Main Street Brown Ale (Harbor City Brewing, Wisconsin); Michigan Mild (Rochester Mills, Michigan); Nut Brown Ale (Weinkeller Brewpub, Illinois); Nut Brown Ale (Arcadia Brewing, Michigan); Pub Brown Ale (Sprecher Brewing, Wisconsin).

English Bitter and Pale Ale

The daily beer of England. Walk into any English pub, order a pint of beer, and you will almost certainly get a bitter. The names English bitter and English pale ale are often used synonymously. Bitters are usually the weaker of the two, served on draught (often cask-conditioned), while English pale ales are typically stronger, higher hopped, more aggressively carbonated, and served bottled. Bitters come in three types: *Ordinary Bitter*, *Special or Best Bitter*, and *Extra Special Bitter*. Robustness of flavor, body, and bitterness tend to increase along with the alcohol levels as you progress from ordinary bitters to an extra special. English bitters and pale ales tend to be less aggressively hopped than their American pale ale counterparts. *Classic examples:* Fuller's London Pride (Special Bitter) and Bass Ale (English Pale Ale).

Recommended Great Lakes examples: Brewhouse E.S.B. (Royal Oak Brewery, Michigan); Dan's Best Bitter (New Glarus Brewing,

Wisconsin); Doc's E.S.B. (Big Buck Brewery, Michigan); English E.S.B. (Detroit Brew Factory, Michigan); E.S.B. (Goose Island Brewing, Illinois); E.S.B. (Weinkeller Brewpub, Illinois); Lake Superior E.S.B. (Arcadia Brewing, Michigan); Moon Dog Ale (Great Lakes Brewing, Ohio); Pierce's Pale Ale (Founders Hill Brewing, Illinois); Plaza Extra Pale Ale (Lafayette Brewing, Indiana).

India Pale Ale (I.P.A.)
Super-premium pale ales ranging from 5-7.5% ABV. This style dates back to the late eighteenth century during the British colonization of India. All those British troops needed beer and the "regular" beer of the time couldn't stand up to the long journey. Innovation is often born of difficulty, and soon I.P.A. was developed to solve the problem. They were brewed to be very high in alcohol and were very aggressively hopped, both of which helped to preserve the precious cargo. The style obviously caught on and even today it is one of the favorite styles of American beer lovers. American-style India Pale Ales provide a showcase for American hop varieties. *Classic examples:* Anchor Liberty Ale and Sierra Nevada Celebration Ale.
Recommended Great Lakes examples: Cask Conditioned Sacred Cow I.P.A. (Arbor Brewing, Michigan); Cornerstone I.P.A. (Rochester Mills Beer Company, Michigan); Crazy Legs India Pale Ale (Brewhouse Pub & Grille, Ohio); Get Fuggled I.P.A. (North Peak Brewing, Michigan); I.P.A. (Goose Island Brewing, Illinois); I.P.A. (Michigan Brewing, Michigan); I.P.A. (Weinkeller Brewpub, Illinois); India Pale Ale (Arcadia Brewing, Michigan); Mad Hatter (New Holland Brewing, Michigan); Potters Run I.P.A. (Great Dane Pub & Brewing, Wisconsin); Snowshovel I.P.A. (Diamondback Brewery, Ohio); Two Hearted Ale (Kalamazoo Brewing, Michigan); Weeping Hog I.P.A. (Lafayette Brewing, Indiana); Old No. 85 (Lafayette Brewing, Indiana).

Porter

This style was developed in the early eighteenth century in England and is thought of as the precursor to the modern stout. Its origin, in 1722, is credited to a London brewer, Ralph Harwood. Harwood's new beer, which he called "Entire," was designed to mimic the flavor of a mixture of beers (pale ale, fermenting brown ale, and aged brown ale) which was very popular among the London porters of the time. The new beer was a great success and soon was simply known as a porter. In the early nineteenth century, Arthur Guinness began calling a porter he was brewing at his Dublin brewery an "Extra Stout Porter." Ultimately this "stout porter" became simply Guinness Stout. Today porters are a rather loosely defined style and are very popular in American microbreweries. Generally speaking, if a brewery offers both a porter and stout, the stout will be the stronger of the two. American porters tend to be medium-bodied with considerable malt character, often roasty and chocolaty. English porters tend to emphasize a caramel malt character, while American examples are more likely to be chocolaty. *Classic examples:* Anchor Porter and Samuel Smith's Taddy Porter. *Recommended Great Lakes examples:* Bell's Porter (Kalamazoo Brewing, Michigan); Black Earth Porter (Great Dane Pub & Brewing, Wisconsin); Cask Conditioned Milestone Porter (Arbor Brewing, Michigan); Cool Mule Porter (Crooked River Brewing, Ohio); Edmund Fitzgerald Porter (Great Lakes Brewing, Ohio); Founders Porter (Canal Street Brewing, Michigan); Honey Porter (Motor City Brewing Works, Michigan); King's Cross Porter (Robert Thomas Brewing, Michigan); Kourage (New Holland Brewing, Michigan); Night Train Porter (Brewhouse Pub & Grille, Ohio); Olde Smoked Porter (Arcadia Brewing, Michigan); Pigskin Porter (Detroit Brew Factory, Michigan); Peninsula Porter (Michigan Brewing, Michigan); Pitsaw Porter (Minocqua Brewing, Wisconsin).

Stout

This style is most accurately seen as several subtypes. When most people think of a stout they think of an *Irish Dry Stout*: Made famous by the classic Guinness Stout, dry stouts are characterized by a malty body and a distinctively dry and roasty bitter finish. They are nearly black in color with ruby hues. Significant variability in malt and hop levels exists in the many fine examples of this style. Oftentimes these beers are served via a nitrogen tap, which imparts a rich, creamy body and head to the beer. *Oatmeal Stout*: This style of stout is brewed with a portion of rolled or flaked oats, which tends to impart a smooth silky character to the beer. *Sweet Stout*: Sometimes referred to as "cream" or "milk" stouts. A sweet and full-body, often the result of adding lactose or other unfermentable sugar, characterizes this style. A fine example is Mackeson XXX Stout. *Imperial Stout*: Also known as a Russian Imperial Stout since it was originally brewed in England and exported to Russia. Imperial stouts are the most intense of the breed, usually exhibiting high alcohol levels (7-10% ABV or higher) complex fruity-esters, and rich malty flavors. *Classic examples:* Samuel Smith's Oatmeal Stout and Imperial Stout.

Recommended Great Lakes examples: Bell's Kalamazoo Stout (Kalamazoo Brewing, Michigan); Big Stone Stout (Bloomington Brewing, Indiana); Black Angus Oatmeal Stout, Digby's Irish Stout (Lafayette Brewing, Indiana); Bourbon County Stout (Goose Island Brewing, Illinois); Earl Spit Stout (Dragonmead Microbrewery, Michigan); Emerald Isle Stout (Great Dane Pub & Brewing, Wisconsin); Faricy-Fest Irish Stout (Arbor Brewing, Michigan); Five Springs Oatmeal Stout (Mickey Finn's Brewery, Illinois); Irish Stout (Sprecher Brewing, Wisconsin); Lake Effect Stout (Roffey Brewing, Michigan); Lake Trout Stout (Boyne River Brewing, Michigan); Locomotive Stout (Flatlanders Brewing, Illinois); Main Street Steamboat Stout (Main Street Brewing, Ohio); Starboard Stout (Arcadia Brewing, Michigan); Stout (Traverse Brewing, Michigan); Triple Nickel Irish Stout (Prairie Rock Brewing, Illinois).

Strong Ale

The term "strong ale" can be used to describe any ale of considerable strength, but most often it refers to a potent English-style ale.

There are two types, Old Ale and Barley Wine. *Old Ale*: An English-style dark ale. The style is rather loosely defined, but most examples are rather strong (upwards of 8.5% ABV), medium copper colored, and full-bodied. Usually they exhibit malty sweetness, some fruitiness, and a clear hop counterbalance. *Barley Wine*: The king of ales. Full-bodied, with a rich residual malty sweetness that is usually countered by aggressive hop bitterness. Very complex, with high alcohol levels and fruity esters, often exhibiting a strong vinous character. Some bottled varieties can benefit from aging. These beers can have alcohol levels reaching upwards of 12% ABV. Both of these potent styles are offered primarily during the winter months to help stave off the cold. *Classic examples:* Theakston's Old Peculiar (Old Ale), Young's Old Nick, Anchor Old Foghorn.

Recommended Great Lakes examples: Auld Curiosity Ale (Barley's Brewing, Ohio); Expedition Stout, Third Coast Old Ale (Kalamazoo Brewing, Michigan); Jackhammer Old Ale (Arbor Brewing, Michigan); Two Fisted Old Ale (King Brewing, Michigan).

Belgian Ales

Only a handful of Great Lakes breweries are currently producing Belgian-style beers. A pity, as these are some of the most flavorful, distinctive, and enjoyable beers of the world. Although volumes can be written about Belgian ales, I will only touch on the few styles that are brewed in the Midwest.

Belgian Wheat (Wit) Beer

Brewed with unmalted wheat in addition to the barley malt. Tradition has this style of beer spiced with coriander and orange peel, although this is not always the case in practice. A distinctive fruitiness is generally present in this style. Usually served unfiltered and somewhat cloudy. *Classic examples:* Hoegaarden and Celis White.

Recommended Great Lakes examples: Belgian Wit (Big Rock Chop & Brew House, Michigan); Belgian Wit (Great Dane Pub & Brewing, Wisconsin); Transcendental Wheat Beer (Harbor City Brewing, Wisconsin); Zoomer Wit (New Holland Brewing, Michigan).

Lambic
Brewed with unmalted wheat and barley malt, and naturally fermented with wild yeast strains. Interestingly, rather than using the freshest hops available as is the custom in brewing, lambic hops are aged anywhere from one to three years. These aged hops are highly oxidized and used solely for their still-remaining antibacterial properties. Lambic beer is extraordinarily complex, fruity, and often intensely sour and acetic. A blended version of aged and young lambic beer is called *Gueuze-Lambic*. Lambic beers are often mixed with fruit to balance their sourness. *Kriek* (made with cherries) and *Framboise* (made with raspberries) are the most common. *Classic producers:* Boon, Cantillon, Girardin, Lindemans.
Recommended Great Lakes examples: Wisconsin Belgian Red Brand Cherry, Raspberry Tart (New Glarus Brewing, Wisconsin); Cranberry Lambic (Diamondback Brewery, Ohio).

Trappist Ales
To be truly called "Trappist," a beer must brewed at one of the six Benedictine monasteries of the Trappist order that brew beer. These monasteries are Chimay, Orval, Rochefort, Westmalle, Westvleteven, and La Trappe. La Trappe is located in the Netherlands; the rest are in Belgium. Beers that are brewed elsewhere and mimic the "Trappist ale" style are generally called "Abbey" beers or "Trappist-Style" beers. If you run across such a beer in the Midwest, it will most likely be either a Dubbel or a Tripel. *Dubbel*: These beers are usually rich and malty, medium to full-bodied, and a dark amber or brown in color. Chocolaty, roasty, and nutty malt characteristics are common, as is some fruitiness, and virtually no detectable hop contribution. *Tripel*: These beers are significantly lighter colored than Dubbels. Brewed with the addition of candi sugar, tripels can be very high in alcohol, upwards of 10% ABV. The flavor tends to be a mix of a sweetness, alcohol, fruitiness, and

a dry spiciness reminiscent of cloves or cinnamon. *Classic examples:* La Trappe Dubbel, and Tripel.

Recommended Great Lakes examples: Fat Abbot Belgian Tripel (Arbor Brewing, Michigan); Dubbel Dragon Ale, Final Absolution Belgian Style Trippel (Dragonmead Microbrewery, Michigan).

Scottish Ales

Generally these beers are maltier and less aggressively hopped than British ales. They are often brewed with "peat-smoked" malts, providing a warm, smoky characteristic. Scottish ales are sometimes named after an old currency of England, the shilling. For example, a beer that would sell for 80 shillings to the barrel would be called an 80 shilling ale. Scottish ales are still rather uncommon in American breweries and often are brewed as a limited availability specialty beer.

Scottish ales have several subtypes. *Light Ale (60 shilling)*: The lightest form of Scottish ale. Light-bodied, very low hop bitterness. *Heavy Ale (70 shilling)*: Maltiness is the dominant flavor. *Scottish Export Ale (80 shilling)*: Stronger than the 70 shilling, with similar characteristics. *Scotch Ale (90 shilling)*: Extra strong Scottish ale. Very malty and full-bodied, often with peat-smoked malt character and alcohol flavor components. Alcohol content can be as high as 8%. *Classic producer:* Caledonian Brewing Co.

Recommended Great Lakes examples: 60 Shilling Scotch Ale, 90 Shilling Scotch Export Ale (Dragonmead Microbrewery, Michigan); MacLenny's Scottish Ale (Barley's Brewing, Ohio); 80 Shilling Scottish Ale (Arbor Brewing, Michigan).

German Ales

Altbier

Altbier refers to an old style of beer in Germany. The term is often used to describe any pre-lager German-style beer. These beers are fermented with ale yeast at warm temperatures and cold conditioned (lagered) for a couple weeks.

Recommended Great Lakes examples: Altbier (Kraftbräu Brewery,

Michigan); German Ale (Brewery Creek Brewing, Wisconsin); Olde No. 22 German Alt (Arbor Brewing, Michigan).

Berliner Weiss

The lightest of German-style wheat beers, this style is known for a strong "lactic" sourness or tartness. Often served with a syrup of some type to offer a balance. These beers derive their sourness through the addition of lactobacillus bacteria. Reportedly this style was quite popular in pre-prohibition America. Surprisingly, very few microbreweries are attempting it today.

Dunkel Weizen or Dunkel Weissbier

Literally means "dark-wheat." In addition to the characteristic phenolic and estery components of other German weissbier, Dunkel Weissbier is darker and sweeter, often exhibiting a roasted malt character and a smooth chocolate-like dimension.

Hefe-Weizen or Hefe-Weissbier

The most common German weissbier in Midwest brewpubs. The style is known for its yeasty-cloudy unfiltered appearance, as well as wonderfully complex and intriguing estery (fruity) and phenolic (spicy) characteristics. Flavors of banana, clove, and nutmeg are common. Vanilla-like flavors are exhibited less frequently. These beers are usually brewed with at least 50% wheat malt. Hop characteristics are usually absent. Refreshing and flavorful, this style is ubiquitous in Midwest brewpubs during the summer months; in fact, during those months it's common for various types of wheat beer to make up nearly half of the beer on tap in many brewpubs. *Classic example:* Hacker-Pschorr Weiss.

Recommended Great Lakes examples: Atwater Hefe-Weizen (Atwater Block Brewery, Michigan); Bavarian Bliss Wheat Beer (Arbor Brewing, Michigan); Bavarian Weiss (Weinkeller Brewpub, Illinois); Crop Circle Wheat (Great Dane Pub & Brewing, Wisconsin); Harsen's Hefe-Weizen (North Channel Brewing, Michigan); Nagelweiss Wheat Beer (Dragonmead Microbrewery, Michigan);

Güdenteit Hefe-Weizen (Mickey Finn's Brewery, Illinois); Hefe-Weiss (Sprecher Brewing, Wisconsin).

Kölsch
A type of altbier that originated in Cologne (Köln), Germany. It is top fermented and cold aged, light golden in color with a subtle fruitiness and a soft light malt body.
Recommended Great Lakes examples: Golden Ale (Lighthouse Brewing, Michigan); Summertime Ale (Goose Island Brewing, Illinois).

Kristal Weizen or Kristal Weissbier
A filtered weissbier. Most of the characteristics of the hefe-weissbier apply in this style, with the exception of the cloudy appearance.

Weizenbock or Weissbock
As it sounds, this style is a weissbier married with a bock. Unlike a bock, this style employs a top fermenting weissbier yeast strain. The resulting beer is dark, malty, and strong, and exhibits the same phenolic and estery characteristics of a weissbier. *Classic example:* Shneider Aventinus.

Lagers

American Lager
A very light beer, often brewed with adjuncts such as corn and rice. Hop aroma and flavor are typically low. Usually aggressively carbonated. *Classic example:* Budweiser
Recommended Great Lakes examples: Stevens Point Special (Stevens Point Brewery, Wisconsin).

American Light Lager
Remarkably light, watery beers. Corn and rice are often used as cheap adjuncts to malted barley. Maltiness is very low and hop characteristics are virtually absent. Aggressively carbonated. A

shockingly popular style of beer. *Classic example:* Bud Light. *Recommended Great Lakes examples:* Founders Light Lager (Founders Hill Brewing, Illinois).

Bock

The popular myth that bock beers are derived from what was left at the bottom of the kettle could not be further from the truth. These beers are brewed from scratch with the same quality ingredients as other styles. Bock beer comes in three main varieties: *Bock, Helles Bock/Maibock*, and the strong *Doppelbock*. *Bock*: Medium to full-bodied, with an evident sweet malty balance. Usually a fairly dark ruby-brown. Alcohol content can reach over 7%. *Helles Bock/ Maibock*: Paler in color than traditional bock beers. *Doppelbock*: Full-bodied and very malty sweet, often with alcohol flavor complexities. Hop bitterness is low. Doppelbock (or double bock) beers are often named with an "-ator" suffix, in honor of the original doppelbock, the Paulaner Salvator.

Recommended Great Lakes examples: Hinterland Maple Bock (Green Bay Brewing, Wisconsin); Terminator Doppelbock, Uskratsch Mai Bock (Arbor Brewing, Michigan); Berghoff Famous Bock Beer (Joseph Huber Brewing, Wisconsin); Point Bock (Stevens Point Brewery, Wisconsin).

California Common

A style of beer indigenous to America. It is made using bottom fermenting lager yeast, but the beer is fermented at the warmer temperatures typically associated with ales. Often cold conditioned (lagered). The resulting hybrid has some characteristics of both ales and lagers, and is often referred to simply as "Steam Beer." The Anchor Brewing Company holds a trademark on the term "Steam Beer" and theirs is the only beer that can bear that name.

Dortmunder Export

A nicely balanced beer, bigger bodied and less hoppy than a pilsner, drier than a Munich helles, and marginally stronger than both.

Classic example: Dortmunder Union Export
Recommended Great Lakes examples: Dortmunder Gold (Great Lakes Brewing, Ohio).

Märzen-Oktoberfest

Traditionally these beers are brewed in March and aged (lagered) until their unveiling during Oktoberfest. Copper colored, with a malty sweet, medium to full body, often finishing with a pleasant, dry spiciness. Similar to Vienna-style lagers, but stronger and maltier.

Munich Dunkel

Dunkel is a German word for dark. These are malty dark lagers with low to moderate hop bitterness, usually exhibiting roasted malt and chocolate-like characteristics.
Recommended Great Lakes examples: East Side Dark (Lakefront Brewery, Wisconsin); Frogtown Dunkel (Maumee Bay Brewing, Ohio); Genuine Dark Beer (Joseph Huber Brewing, Wisconsin); Munich Dark (Capital Brewing, Wisconsin).

Munich Helles

The German word hell means, "pale" or "light." As you might guess, this style of beer is a Munich-style pale colored lager. A nicely balanced beer, featuring a wonderfully soft maltiness and low bitterness. Fuller bodied than a pilsner. Most American microbrewery (especially brewpub) lagers are variants of this style. Sometimes described as an "all day" beer, in reference to their easy drinkability.
Recommended Great Lakes examples: Berghoff Original Lager Beer (Joseph Huber Brewing, Wisconsin); Krausen Hell (Atwater Brewing, Michigan); Social Climber Light Lager (Local Color Brewing, Michigan).

Pilsner

Generally divided into two main types, *German* style and *Bohemian* style. Classic examples of the German style have high hop bitterness, a well attenuated light to medium body, fresh hop aroma, and a dense foamy head. They usually finish quite dry, sometimes salty. Bohemian style pilsners, sometimes called a Czechoslovakian pilsner, are similar to the German style but tend to be fuller-bodied and maltier. Saaz hops are a favorite in the Bohemian style. *Classic examples:* Bitburger (German), Pilsner Urquell (Bohemian). *Recommended Great Lakes examples:* Atwater Pilsner (Atwater Brewing, Michigan); Gasthaus Pils (Mickey Finn's Brewery, Illinois); No Parking Pilsner (Arbor Brewing, Michigan); Peck's Pilsner (Great Dane Pub & Brewing, Wisconsin); Pilsner (Michigan Brewing, Michigan); Smooth Talker Pilsner (Local Color Brewing, Michigan); Special Pilsner (Capital Brewing, Wisconsin).

Schwarzbier
A German style that literally means "black beer." These are just beginning to be offered more frequently at American microbreweries.
Recommended Great Lakes examples: Black Bavarian (Sprecher Brewing Co., Wisconsin); Dark Horse Special Reserve Black Bier (Dark Horse Brewing, Michigan).

Vienna
Light copper-red color. Soft, malty aroma and flavor, balanced by a perceivable bitterness. Often has a light, slightly dry spiciness. Closely related to Märzen-Oktoberfest style lagers, though lighter in body and maltiness. *Classic example:* Dos Equis Amber. *Recommended Great Lakes examples:* Eliot Ness (Great Lakes Brewing, Ohio); Riverwest Stein Beer (Lakefront Brewery, Wisconsin); Special Amber (Sprecher Brewing, Wisconsin).

187

Specialty Beers

These beers are usually brewed as seasonals.

Christmas Ale

Usually these are spiced beers, often strong ones. Raisins, nutmeg, cinnamon, honey, maple sugar, ginger root, caraway, juniper, and coriander are just some of the common ingredients.

Recommended Great Lakes examples: Bell's Eccentric Ale (Kalamazoo Brewing, Michigan); Christmas Ale (Barley's Brewing, Ohio); St. Brigid's Strong Ale (O'Gradys Brewery & Pub, Illinois); Christmas Ale (Great Lakes Brewing, Ohio).

Coffee or Java Beers

Rapidly becoming a popular style in American microbreweries. Usually coffee is added to dark, robust beers such as porters and stouts. Examples of this style can range from a subtle roasty and coffee character, to an extremely robust and intense coffee assault.

Classic example: Redhook Doubleblack Stout.

Recommended Great Lakes examples: Buffalo Jump Stout (Copper Canyon Brewery, Michigan); Java Stout (Kalamazoo Brewing, Michigan).

Pumpkin Ale

An increasingly popular beer offered in microbreweries. Obviously a fall beer, served around Halloween. These beers are brewed with pumpkin and are usually spiced with nutmeg and cinnamon. They vary widely in strength and flavor.

Recommended Great Lakes examples: Ichabod (New Holland Brewing, Michigan); The Great Pumpkin Ale (North Channel Brewing, Michigan).

10 INGREDIENTS FOR
AN EXCELLENT BREWERY

1. True-to-Style Beers

While brewing true-to-style is actually a simple concept, it is surprising how many breweries fail to practice it. Too many breweries simply offer watered-down versions of each style they brew. Often these beers share very little in common with the styles they are said to represent. Such brewing practices seem to be an effort to please the palate of the average American light lager drinker. A better strategy would be to offer a few excellent examples of naturally light styles for the novice drinker. There are many such styles to choose from. The result is a brewery that satisfies the novice beer drinker and beer aficionados as well. The best breweries do just that. They brew beers from a wide range of styles, each brewed with a respect and caring, and all brewed true-to-style.

2. Beers of Distinction

Distinctive beers are like distinctive wines, or foods. We remember them. Some quality they possess enables them to stand out from the pack. The best breweries offer such an experience; beers that simply cannot be had anywhere else. Whether it is an interestingly hopped I.P.A., an alcohol packed winter warmer, or an incredibly unique fruit beer, a distinctive beer of some type will be found in any great brewery. New Glarus of Wisconsin and Kalamazoo Brewing in Michigan certainly come to mind.

3. Cask-Conditioned Ales

The traditional beer of England is slowly gaining acceptance here in the United States. Many ale-producing breweries throughout the Great Lakes region are now offering cask-conditioned versions of their ales. Cold temperatures and aggressive carbonation can cover up many subtle flavors and characteristics a beer may possess. Cask-conditioned ales are served warmer (usually around 55° Fahrenheit) and are gently carbonated by natural yeast activity. The resulting beers are soft and silky on the palate and often exhibit a multitude of subtle and complex flavors.

4. Customer Education

Excellent customer education is perhaps one of the most important goals for any microbrewery. Happily, "Beer 101" is taught in one form or another at most of the finest microbreweries and brewpubs in the region. Homebrew clubs, organized beer tastings, or just a well-trained staff can go a long way to increasing customer understanding and ultimate enjoyment of the various styles of beer that are offered.

5. Annually Anticipated Seasonal Beers

Recurring seasonal beers are an excellent and appreciated way for breweries to create excitement about their beer. Over time, these beers generate a loyal following and their yearly arrival becomes eagerly anticipated. Springtime bocks, summer pilsners, holiday beers, pumpkin ales, winter warmers, and others can be found at the finest breweries all over the Great Lakes region.

6. Involvement with the Community

More and more breweries, especially those in small towns, are seeing the value in a close relationship with the community. Many of the best breweries participate heavily in community activities, ranging from various charity events to sponsoring and organizing yearly beer festivals. Others offer community-oriented programs, such as "designated drivers eat free" nights, to encourage responsible drinking.

7. Proper Glassware

In most European pubs and beer cafes, each style of beer is served in its own appropriate style of glassware. It sounds picky, but the right glassware can significantly enhance the enjoyment of virtually any beer. Thankfully, at a growing number of breweries the standard 16-ounce pint glass is no longer used exclusively and regardless of the beer style.

8. Proper Temperature

There are few things less appealing than a Pilsner at room temperature or an English ale served at near freezing. Because the beer drinking population in the United States consumes primarily lagers, the tendency at microbreweries is to serve all their beer at relatively cold lager temperatures. While this practice eliminates the "hey, this beer is warm" complaint, it also can be devastating to the enjoyment of a complex ale. The best breweries serve each of their beers at the proper temperature for the style. Equally important, the best breweries react to the "hey, this beer is warm" complaint as an opportunity to educate, not capitulate.

9. Cook with Beer

The best brewpubs and microbrewery-restaurants view cooking with their own house beer as an opportunity to create menu items as distinctive and unique as the beer they brew. Commonly offered are beer batter fries, sauces and soups made with beer, and a variety of unique entrees.

10. Avoid "Themes"

This is admittedly more subjective than the rest, but I have a problem with "theme breweries." They exist in many forms, such as the "cat theme" where every beer and menu item derives its name from some feline. Others examples include Australian, nautical, firehouse, prison, dog, train station, and hunting themes. Sure, they can be cute sometimes, and one or two might make good beer, but I have noticed that very few of the best breweries use the theme gimmick. Somehow, the quality of their beer alone is enough to bring them success. Strangely satisfying, isn't it?

GLOSSARY OF BEER TERMS

ABV: Alcohol by volume. Expressed as a percentage.

ABW: Alcohol by weight. Expressed as a percentage.

Ale: Ales are the most ancient of brews, with a history dating back to ancient Egypt. Made with top fermenting yeast, ales are fermented at relatively warm temperatures.

Attenuation: The extent to which yeast consumes fermentable sugars.

Barley: The principal grain, and one of the four basic ingredients, of beer.

Barrel: A unit of measure equaling 31 gallons.

Beer Engine: The most familiar method of serving cask-conditioned ale in England. A beer engine is a simple suction pump operated by a tall-handled handpump. When the handle is drawn, the engine "pulls" a predetermined amount of beer from the cask, often a half-pint of beer for each pull. Beer engines are also referred to as "handpulls."

Black & Tan: Usually an equal mixture of a house dark and light beer, most often, a stout or porter mixed with pale or red ale. A classic example of a black & tan is the combination *Guinness Stout* and *Harp Lager*.

Body: A term that describes the level of perceived heaviness or thickness on the palate. Sweet, thick and rich beers, like some stouts and doppelbocks, are often described as "big-bodied" or "full-bodied."

Bottle Conditioning: A practice of adding a priming agent (sugar or wort), and yeast to freshly bottled beer. The bottled beer is then given time to "condition." During the conditioning process the yeast consumes the additional sugars and naturally carbonates the beer. Some bottle-conditioned beers can continue to improve with age, sometimes for years.

Brew-on-Premise (B.O.P.): Some microbreweries also offer a service called brew-on-premise. These breweries allow customers to come in and brew their own recipes (or use the brewery's own recipes) on small scale professional brewing equipment. For a full description of the process on the Internet, surf to *The Brew on Premises Beer Pages* at: http://www.tcel.com/~gobrew/

Brewpub: The specific laws vary from state to state. For the purposes of this guide, a brewpub is a small brewery that serves the majority of its beer in house. Virtually all brewpubs in the Great Lakes region sell beer to go in the form of growlers. Some also sell beer to go in "party pigs," quarter- and half-barrels.

Cask Conditioned Ale: The traditional beer of England. Cask conditioning is quite similar to bottle conditioning. A priming sugar, clarifying agent, and sometimes dry hops (see *dry hopping*) are added to the filled cask. At the conclusion of this second fermentation the beer is naturally carbonated, usually to a low level. The resulting beer is extremely smooth and very easy drinking.

Dry Hopping: The addition of dry hops to fermenting or conditioning beer. This practice provides additional hop character and aroma in the final beer.

Esters: A by-product of fermentation that can produce fruity aromas and characteristics. Fruity esters are more often found in ales due to warmer fermentation and the natural characteristics of ale yeast.

Fermentation: The breakdown of sugars into carbon dioxide and alcohol by yeast.

Firkin: A small wooden barrel or cask with a 1/4 barrel capacity.

Growler: A half-gallon glass jug that has become the standard "to-go" container of brewpubs.

Hops: The dried flowers of this twining vine plant, containing bitter and aromatic oils, are one of the four basic ingredients of beer. They are the "spice" in beer, providing a bitter balance against the sweet barley malt. Hops come in many varieties. Some, referred to as "noble hops," are prized for their delicate aromas and flavors.

I.B.U.: International bittering units. A measure of hop bitterness.

Krausening: The addition of a small amount of "young," still fermenting wort to a fully fermented beer. The addition of these sugars prompts a secondary fermentation, which naturally carbonates the beer.

Lager: Beers produced with bottom fermenting yeast, and usually fermented at relatively cold temperatures.

Microbrewery: The specific laws vary from state to state. For the purposes of this guide, a microbrewery is a small brewery that produces less than 15,000 barrels of beer annually and may sell most of its beer off-premises. Most microbreweries distribute their beer in bottles and various keg accounts. Breweries that are categorized as microbreweries in this guide do not offer on-site consumption except as small samples. (See also *Microbrewery-Taproom* and *Microbrewery-Restaurant*.)

Microbrewery-Taproom: A microbrewery, as defined by this guide, with a small taproom attached for serving draught beer on-site. Usually snacks and token food items are available, such as popcorn, pretzels, nachos, or peanuts.

Microbrewery-Restaurant: A microbrewery, as defined by this guide, with a full restaurant attached that serves house-brewed beer.

Mouthfeel: The texture, consistency, or viscosity of a beer as perceived in the mouth.

Nose: The olfactory experience provided by a beer's aroma.

Party Pig: A small 2.25-gallon keg. Pressurized and served via tap.

Phenolic: A spicy or clove-like flavor that is appropriate in German Weissbier. Phenolic can also describe a medicinal or chemical flavor that sometimes occurs in beer, usually due to contamination.

Regional Brewery: A brewery that produces from 15,000 to 1 million barrels of beer annually. (See also *Regional Brewery-Taproom* and *Regional Brewery-Restaurant.*)

Regional Brewery-Taproom: A regional brewery, as defined by this guide, with a small taproom attached for serving draught beer on-site. Usually snacks and token food items are available, such as popcorn, pretzels, nachos, or peanuts.

Regional Brewery-Restaurant: A regional brewery, as defined by this guide, with a full restaurant attached that serves their own house-brewed beer.

Reinheitsgebot: The German Purity Law of 1516. It states that the only lawful ingredients in the production of beer are water, malt (barley and wheat), hops, and yeast.

Session Beer: A term used to describe an easy drinking and low alcohol beer that one can drink throughout an evening without becoming too inebriated. A session beer is most often a light English or Scottish ale.

Water: Probably best known for it role as one of the basic four ingredients of beer. Often overlooked, water quality and mineral composition can have a dramatic impact on the finished beer.

Wort: An unfermented mixture of water, sugars (principally from malted barley), and hops.

Yeast: One of the four basic ingredients of beer. A single cell organism that is capable of metabolizing sugars into carbon dioxide and alcohol.

INDEX OF BREWERIES